Shipwrecks and Nautical Lore

of

Boston Harbor

SHIPWRECKS AND NAUTICAL LORE

of

BOSTON HARBOR

*A Mariner's Chronicle of
More Than 100 Shipwrecks, Heroic Rescues, Salvage,
Treasure Tales, Island Legends, and Maritime Anecdotes*

by

Robert F. Sullivan

The
Globe
Pequot
Press

Chester, Connecticut

Quotations on pages 41, 102, and 124 are copyright © 1896, 1936, and 1951 respectively and are reprinted courtesy of *The Boston Globe.*

Copyright © 1990 by Robert F. Sullivan

Library of Congress Cataloging-in-Publication Data

Sullivan, Robert F.
    Shipwrecks and nautical lore of Boston Harbor: a mariner's chronicle of more than 100 shipwrecks, heroic rescues, salvage, treasure tales, island legends, and mar-itime anecdotes/by Robert F. Sullivan.—1st ed.
      p. cm.
    ISBN 0-87106-497-9
    1. Shipwrecks—Massachusetts—Boston Bay.   I. Title.
  G525.S894 1990   90-32075
  974.4—dc20   CIP

Manufactured in the United States of America
First Edition/First Printing

This chronicle is dedicated to the memory of G. Stinson Lord of Weymouth, Massachusetts, a man who taught the author about the intrigue of history, the fascination of exploring, and the artistry of God in creations of nature.

The author deeply appreciates the kind assistance received from all points of the compass in researching material for this chronicle.

The Nancy *on Nantasket Beach with scores of paying sightseers*
(Courtesy: Peabody Museum of Salem)

Contents

THE OUTER HARBOR

Harding's Ledge Shipwrecks

Outer-Islands Shipwrecks

THE MIDDLE HARBOR

Middle-Islands Shipwrecks

BOSTON LIGHT.

THE INNER HARBOR

Boston and Inner-Islands Shipwrecks

APPENDIXES

Prologue

⟨knot ornament⟩

The Boston Harbor depths conceal the vestiges of a surprising number of historical and intriguing shipwrecks. Truly, the harbor is a classic link in the "stern and rock-bound" New England coast, a chain of bristling ledges, unsheltered islands, and exposed beaches. Almost all the perils that guard the approaches to the Port of Boston are places hallowed by mariners who perished with their vessels.

Unpredictable weather can suddenly transfigure these waters from breathless calm to howling fury, when the waves roll for the high stakes of human lives. The noble and the brave can be humbled by the majesty of the sea's occasional violence. At other times, the serenity and radiance of the harbor appear as if the Almighty is cupping it in the hollow of His hands.

A great many disasters were caused by gales that slash across Massachusetts Bay through the harbor archipelago; torrents of wind sweep next over the shallow inner basins, such as Dorchester Bay, and storm the heights of Shawmut, the Indian name for Boston. Legions of sailors have heard the wind wail through taut rigging as if giving voice to shipmates lost with doomed vessels.

During the 1800s particularly, local newspaper columns relating to ship arrivals and clearances were punctuated with obituaries for wrecked craft. In *Historic Storms of New England,* Sidney Perley advises that in the gale of September 9, 1815, "hundreds of vessels were lost, the newspapers of that time saying they had not enough space to record the marine disasters."

Isaac M. Small, for fifty years Marine Reporting Agent for the Boston Chamber of Commerce, voiced sadness over such tragedies: "Out there across yonder bar, where you see the waters curl and break into a ripple, forming a white line against the blue sea beyond, lies the sunken and sea-

BOSTON HARBOUR

From the Survey of A.S. Wadsworth Esq.U.S.N.

and the Chart of Des Barres.

Statute Miles

Nautical Miles

Common tides rise 10 feet. Spring tides 13 feet.
though frequently varied by the winds.
High water at full & Change at XI.⁴

Drawn by E.Blunt.   Published by E&G.W.Blunt. New York .18

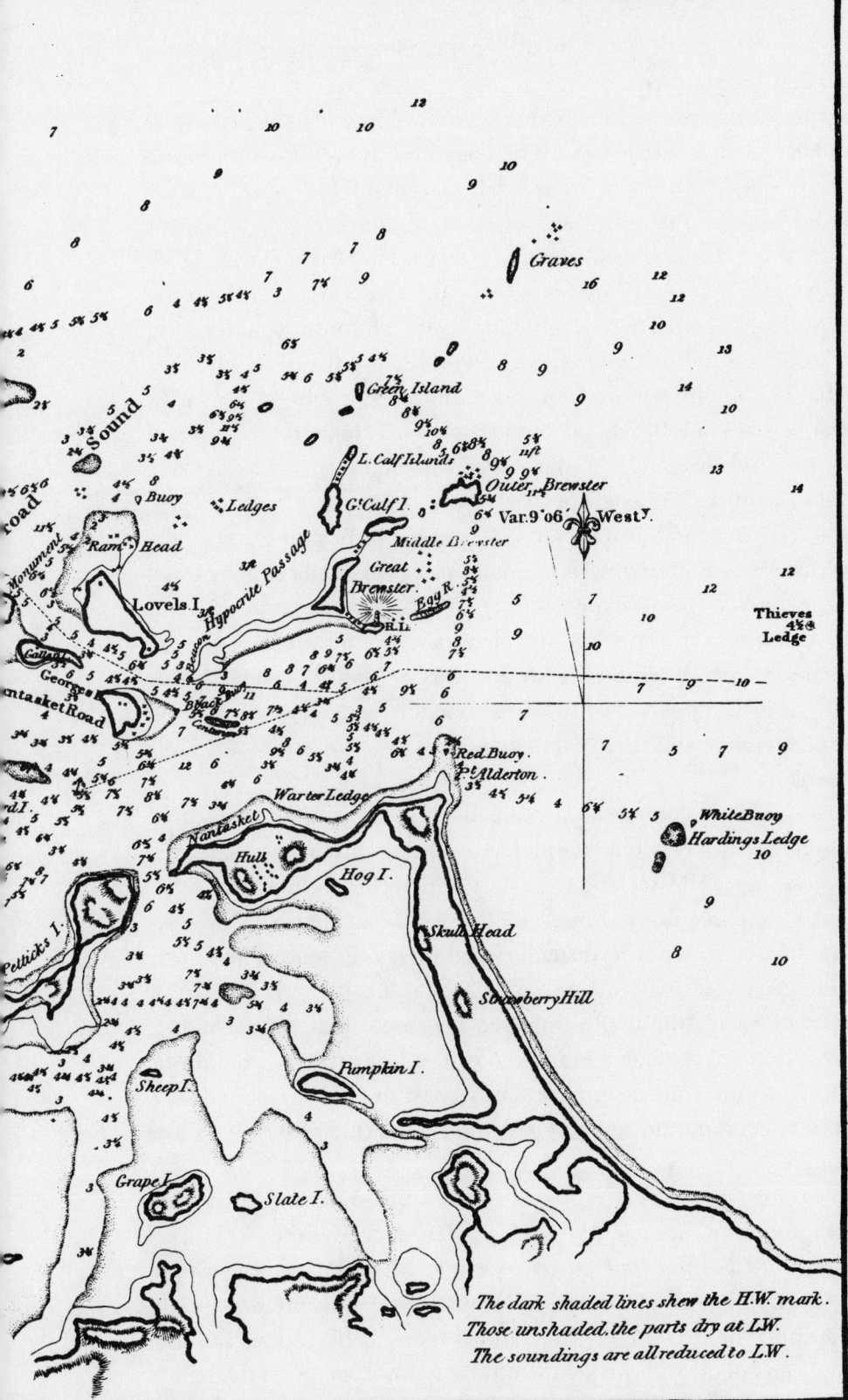

The dark shaded lines shew the H.W. mark.
Those unshaded, the parts dry at L.W.
The soundings are all reduced to L.W.

W. Hooker, Engraver.

washed hull of the once stately ship; in that sparless hull and the rotting sand-covered timbers you cannot recognize the majestic vessel that only a few short years ago sat out there in all her splendor, and her strong sides seemed to defy the elements."

The countless harbor calamities are registered by journalists, as in the *Boston Post* of March 14, 1895, where we learn that retired Captain Moses B. Tower of Hull, one of the oldest officially appointed harbor wreck masters, "has a record of floating 1,700 vessels of all descriptions during his career." Mr. Tower's zealous activities after the gale of December 29, 1853, reported in the *Port of Boston Marine Journal*, included salvage work on the brig *Choctaw*, ashore on Hull Beach, laden with cotton and hides; brig *Waterwitch*, with a cargo of hard pine, driven up on Toddy Rocks; schooner *Galata*, coal laden, also ashore high on Stony Beach; schooner *John G. Faxon*, stranded at Long Beach, between Strawberry Hill and White Head; and schooner *Whirlwind*, bilged (her bottom opened up) on Man-o'-war Bar, Lovell's Island, with 185 tons of coal.

In those days of wind-driven craft, a shipwreck in Boston Harbor during a nor'easter was as inevitable as the tide. Along the Hull coastline especially, beachcombers could expect to come upon the skeleton of some once fleet messenger of the seas. Like birds of prey, the wreckers—those commercial salvagers of wrecked craft and cargo—had descended upon the victim and picked it clean. The skeletal remains were all that remained of captains' surrendering their commands, first to wind and waves, and then to wreckers.

In hard winters a shipwreck with valuable cargo, especially foodstuffs, was a godsend to Hull residents (Hullonians) and their harbor neighbors. Fishing, lobstering, and wrecking were part of daily life in these domains. No evidence has come down, however, of a vessel ever being decoyed to shore here. In fact, so many townsmen risked their lives to save mariners, it seems inconceivable that anyone would jeopardize his own kinfolk by setting up a disaster. Admittedly, the wreckers might hail with delight a vessel once stranded, but they were never known to turn away from those in distress. Time and time again, the hardy coast dwellers exhibited skill and bravery in bending the oars to pluck their fellow men from the unrelenting combers.

Opportunists among these samaritans would sometimes raise the shipowner's and insurance agent's hackles. A few days after the November 1888 storm, the *Gloucester Daily Times* reported: "Brig *Alice* which drifted out of this harbor Sunday afternoon and went ashore on Nantasket Beach has been stripped of her rigging, cargo and every available thing; even her masts have been cut up and carried off. Nothing now remains of the handsome craft but her hull, and the wreckers will steal that, only give them time enough. Every square inch of copper is stripped from the bottom. It's a tough state of affairs and should be surely investigated and the thieves made to disgorge their ill-gotten booty."

After the British schooner *Ulrica* was stranded in 1896 off Nantasket Beach, ten tenacious but alarmed wreckers had to be taken off the hulk by Massachusetts Humane Society lifesavers when the surf again grew dangerously high.

Those Humane Society volunteers and the U.S. Life Saving Service rescued so many lives and so much property that they swell the annals of heroism around Boston Harbor and along the Massachusetts coast.

Anne Kinnear, chairman of the Hull Historical Commission, points out that the famed Irish poet and patriot John Boyle O'Reilly praised some of the Hull lifesavers in a speech given at the Parker House in Boston in December 1888:

> *Let me speak for the men of Hull—the men who pulled the oars in Captain James' boat—for I have the honor to know every one of them as an old friend. I know that the Jameses themselves are Dutchmen by blood; that the Mitchells are Austrians; that the Popes are Yankees; that the Augustuses are from Rome; and that the Galianos also are Italians. But what of their blood and their race? These brave men are neither Dutch nor Irish—they are Americans. And the men of Hull are types not only of Massachusetts, but of America.*

Owing to the increased reliability of the steam engine, other propulsion methods, and development of radio, radar, and sonar, vessels are no longer entirely at the mercy of the elements. As a result, the frequency of shipwrecks has diminished signficantly. Also, an effective network of aids to navigation has been instituted along the coastline. These include a variety of efficient lighthouses, range lights, fog bell and whistle signals, and buoys. Lighthouses are assigned different illumination patterns and colors to give them characteristics for quick and proper identification. Navigational buoys or unmanned tower structures of intense candlepower are replacing lightships, which can be blown off station by gales. The buoy system has been standardized nationwide, and the technology of modern time encompasses buoys lighted with experimental nuclear-power sources. Navigation with the assistance of orbiting satellites is also a reality. Furthermore, there is a wide variety of state and federal government publications, such as accurate nautical charts, light lists, and tide and current tables.

Seamanship, in other words, has evolved into a concise science aided by highly sophisticated instruments; certified maritime and technical insti-

Schooner Ulrica *stranded on Nantasket Beach* (Courtesy: John P. Richardson, Hingham, Mass.)

tutions are now educating sailors on the varied intricacies of their trade. Ultimately, however, a ship's safety continues to rest in the hands of its captain, who, still alone, must give the orders deciding the fate of a vessel.

Boston Harbor has been the stage for hundreds of maritime dramas over the centuries, since at least 1614. Indeed, the harbor is a burial chamber for an armada of vessels, all sent there by the violent acts of nature—or the irrational nature of man. Paradoxically, a surprising number of vessels and seamen went to their destruction, not on remote stretches of desolate coastline, but within plain view of the Massachusetts State House golden dome.

To comprehend fully the reasons behind these unique shipping pitfalls in the harbor environment, we must examine the conditions that contributed to the calamities.

General Description of Harbor

⚓

Boston Harbor lies within the arms extended by Cape Ann and Cape Cod, which form the portals of Massachusetts Bay. The harbor's general limits stretch in a wide arc seaward from Deer Island, off Winthrop, to Point Allerton in Hull. Shipwrecks associated with Boston embrace an even greater scope: from Winthrop Head to the southernmost part of Nantasket Beach in Hull.

Nantasket Roads, the official main entrance to the harbor, is marked by the towering white pillar of Boston Lighthouse, nestled among the ledges. This traditional channel between Little Brewster (Lighthouse Island) and Point Allerton is a confined funnel for ships, especially on a pitch-black night amid raging winds, beset by bone-chilling cold and surg-

Boston Lighthouse

F. GLEASON, {CORNER BROMFIELD AND TREMONT STS.   BOSTON, SATURDAY, JULY 31, 1852. $2 PER VOLUME. 10 Cts. SINGLE. } VOL. III. No. 5.—WHOLE No. 57.

View of Boston waterfront used as a banner on a period newspaper

ing seas as fusillades of hail rattle down on the deck. Add to this nerve-wracking passage a bit of compass deviation, drift impelled by insidious tidal currents, and perhaps a slight miscalculation in plotting. Such conditions often made the attempt to thread a vessel into this needle-hole of the harbor a fatal end to a long voyage on the very threshold of home port.

With Shag Rocks on the starboard side and swirling currents rushing past Toddy Rocks to port, some incoming mariners were no doubt reminded of the Straits of Messina on the coast of Italy. There a huge rock was thought to be the abode of the mythical monster Scylla, which would seize and wreck passing vessels. Just across the narrow straits off Sicily was a dangerous whirlpool believed to be the home of another terrible creature, Charybdis. For a craft to avoid one danger meant steering at great risk into the jaws of the other.

Nantasket Roads, roughly a mile wide, holds for about a mile and a quarter, but the channel deep enough for vessels is much narrower. We condense the now outmoded description of a clipper ship's inbound course: The helmsman would first steer west through the Roads for about a mile and an eighth, then northwest into The Narrows—a mere quarter mile across—between Bug Lighthouse on False Spit, and George's Island, on which stands the Civil War bastion of Fort Warren, formerly the Gibraltar of Boston Harbor; here the vessel would sail northwest by north between Lovell's Island and Gallop's Island for three-quarters of a mile, until abreast of Nix's Mate on the port side; then a tack northwest toward

View of Hull

the high ground on Deer Island to the Broad Sound channel; she would then change course west one-half north through President's Roads, passing south of Deer Island and north of Long Island and Spectacle Island; then head west-northwest up to Boston, traveling by Governor's Island on the north and Castle Island to the south. More specific sailing directions would refer to the somber shaft of Bunker Hill monument and the State House dome as navigational points.

The harbor is blessed with deep anchorages. Sailing vessels waiting for a commissioned pilot could anchor in Nantasket Roads, two cable lengths from Little Brewster Island, but were not to proceed further. A recommended anchorage was in the Roads, with Nix's Mate "just on" with Gallop's Island and the lighthouse "shut well on" to George's Island. Another place was President's Roads, suitably wide, with a sticky bottom, and within the harbor. This area was contained between Governor's Island Flats and Apple Island Flats on the north, Deer Island on the east, Long Island and Spectacle on the south, and Castle Island and Governor's Island on the west. Refuge under Spectacle Island was convenient for coasters caught in northeast winds.

Nathaniel B. Shurtleff, in his 1891 *Topographical and Historical Description of Boston,* relates: "If the map of the harbor is carefully inspected, the first impression made upon an observer is that of the curious forms nature has given to these various islands; which forms have been most queerly changed by the effects of the currents, and now, with their beaches and projecting points and headlands, present to the eye the most grotesque and amusing shapes." Shurtleff gives a "mnemonic" list of fanciful reasons for island shapes and names.

A Witch's Brew of Hazards

A detailed wreck chart reveals the multitude of risks that threaten the harbor's shipping avenues.

The northern perimeter of Nantasket Roads is studded with sporadic rocky spires and an island patchwork. Separating these are intriguingly named but dangerous waterways such as Flying Place, Hypocrite Channel,

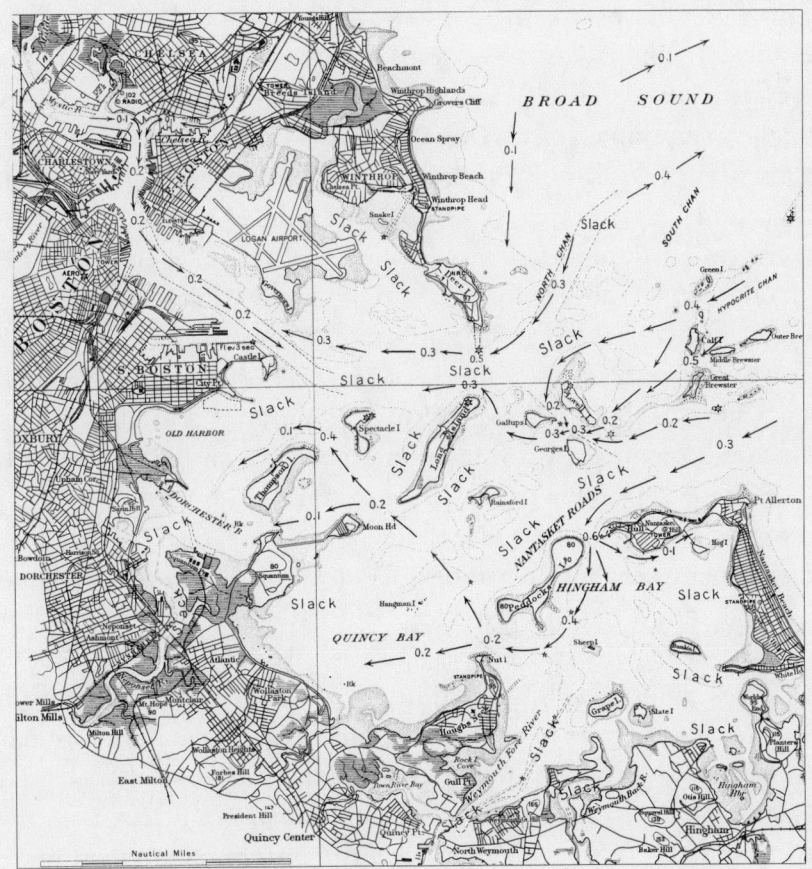

View of harbor and example of complex currents

and Black Rock Passage, which lead toward the inner harbor. Mixed hazards include potent, hidden underwater crags in Broad Sound. Even an experienced skipper could have heart flutters while negotiating the serpentine channels. Sailors claimed some of the waterways were more crooked than Boston streets.

On Nantasket Roads' opposite flank, rock-strewn Stony Beach has witnessed several wrecks. This stretch of mainland shore ranges from Windmill Point on the west, past Stony Beach and Telegraph Hill's erosion-scarred bluffs to Point Allerton, where the waters eddy over perilous gravel bars. From Point Allerton beautiful Nantasket Beach abruptly curves to the south-southeast. Here an observer might visualize Alfred Lord Tennyson's Light Brigade as huge combers roll in like battle lines of cavalry horses while the wind whips back cresting manes. The surf's hollow thundering suggests cannon and pounding hooves.

The ominous forms of Harding's Ledge, Shag Rocks, and even the Graves, with its contemporary granite lighthouse silhouetted against the horizon, stand like tombstones for shattered ships. Other wrecks repose under shifting sand or streaming kelp at shoals such as Man-o'-war Bar, where a leviathan French seventy-four-gun ship has lain since 1782. The geology certainly favors marine disasters. In fact the Devil's Back, a jagged reef in Broad Sound, raked the bottoms from a number of craft.

In times of severe weather, heavy ice sometimes formed out to the borders of the main ship channel. During January 1821, the harbor was filled with vessels encased in ice. The freeze extended several miles from the wharves, and teams transported sled loads of supplies and landed cargoes. It was said to be the hardest winter since 1780. Several craft that were forced ashore when the ice broke up were promptly hauled off.

In the *Boston Advertiser*'s Port of Boston Memoranda for January 29, 1822, we find that the keeper of Boston Light reported on the dangers in freezing water. The brig *Miles Standish* had disappeared, and when last seen "her hull was so completely covered with ice that but for her masts it would have been impossible for anyone to have known it to be a vessel."

In frigid years such as the winters of 1843–44, 1856–57, and 1874–75, ice-glazed rocks were all the more difficult to differentiate from buoys when the channels were frozen over. Underwater ice blocks could also shear off a rudder or keel. At times a ship would arrive in below-freezing temperatures almost wholly encased in frozen spray, making it impossible to work the sails. Icing on braces and bowlines might be as thick as a man's arm, and deadeyes could be immense, big as a barrel.

When the Cunard Line royal steamship *Britannia* left East Boston on February 3, 1844, Boston merchants paid handsomely to keep her on schedule. Avoiding embarrassment from New York competitors meant cutting a canal in the ice approximately 7 miles long and 100 feet wide.

The *Boston Transcript* commented:

> *The harbor presents one of the most animating scenes ever witnessed, being literally covered, as far as the eye can reach, by men, horses and apparatus, and thousands of men and boys upon skates, horses, sleighs, boats upon runners, and tents for the protection and refreshment of the men at work. Several men at the foot of Long Wharf are doing a very clever business taking a toll for the privilege of passing up and down ladders to the ice, one cent being exacted.*

British Mail Steamer coming up Boston Harbor through the ice

This sketch illustrates the skeletal remains of a historical wrecked vessel that was displayed in Boston.

Pirates and Treasure

—≈—

Traditions tell of treasure wrecks that struck during the 1600s and 1700s in the outer harbor. A landlubber adventurer cannot help imagining that these might have been galleons forced northward by violent weather, pirate craft heavy with plunder from the Spanish Main, or privateers that had pounced on richly laden merchantmen.

The thirty-ton bark *Blessing of the Bay*, built in 1631, was the first trading vessel launched in the Mystic River, which flowed into the harbor. She later became our nation's fledgling navy, operating against the increasing threat of eastern-seaboard pirates. The sea wolves, pursuing a Boston-bound sloop, even had the audacity to fire cannon at the intended prize within hailing distance of Outer Brewster Island.

A so-called pirate, Thomas Pound, skipper of the *Rose*, was a skilled cartographer and drew an excellent chart of Boston Harbor about 1685. Suffolk County Court files show that sailors from the *Rose* were indicted for a piratical attack on the *Elinor* in Nantasket Roads on November 21, 1689.

During 1699, the buccaneer Captain William Kidd was apprehended in Boston while toting so much pocket money that his breeches were almost falling down. The captain's financial backers included Lord Bellomont, governor of the Commonwealth. The governor found the partnership embarrassing and decided to sacrifice Kidd, who languished in jail for months, victimized by Boston political piracy. Completing his hatchet job, Bellomont had the captain shipped to England in irons. Following a questionable trial on vague charges, Kidd was dropped through the gallows trapdoor on Execution Dock, London, on May 24, 1701. No one knows what became of his treasure trove.

An 1880s student of Kidd's activities speculated—erroneously—that his treasure ship, the *Quedah*, which mysteriously disappeared from Hispaniola, might have met disaster on the bars off Cape Cod in 1717, bearing a similar-sounding name, *Whydah*. The latter, carrying twenty-three cannon, was commanded by the ill-famed corsair Captain Samuel Bellamy, who perished with 100 of his cohorts. Several survivors were tried and a few necks were stretched by the Boston hangman.

Ironically, a sloop that Governor Samuel Shute dispatched to collect the *Whydah* riches was captured by pirates. Commanded by the governor's representative, Cyprian Southack, once a fellow privateer of Kidd in King William's War, these colonial Keystone Cops allegedly recovered none of the goods. The *Whydah* treasure caused much controversy within the Massachusetts government in 1717, and her potential taxable booty may again whet bureaucratic appetites from Beacon Hill, Boston, to Capitol Hill, Washington.

A few years after the *Whydah* incident, James Franklin, brother of patriot Benjamin Franklin, reportedly was imprisoned by officials for his Boston newspaper commentary about public funds doled out for unproductive expeditions against cutthroats. Franklin had insinuated that freebooters other than those infesting Massachusetts waters were abroad.

Nix's Mate, a diminutive island that long ago eroded into a shoal, stripped for ships' ballast and worn by tides, served as a place for disposing of pirates. Hanging in full view from chains and rattling in the wind, they reminded passing mariners of the penalty for violating Boston's rather tarnished golden rule. These scourges of the sea also dangled from the gibbets on Bird Island, now also obliterated by scouring currents. Others were hanged at the Charlestown Ferry site.

As Boston-bred William Fly was being fitted with a noose, he appealed to masters of vessels "not to be barbarous with their men; for this condition encouraged them to turn to pirating." The *Boston News Letter* of July 14, 1726, stated that "Fly behaved himself very unbecomingly, even to the last." Apparently he was true to the convictions of his trade. Nix's Mate is now identified by a granite obelisk, a navigational marker that, when shrouded in mist, is a sepulchral sight.

Henry David Thoreau visited the harbor at the height of his writing career and sagely observed "isles rapidly wasting away, the sea nibbling voraciously at the continent." Nix's Mate and Bird Island are classic illustrations.

Strange that the isles where cutthroats were executed have all but disappeared from view. The last of the pirate breed to be captured and executed in Boston were Captain Pedro Gilbert and four of his accomplices from the ship *Panda*. They were strung up at the old Suffolk County Jail in 1835.

On the other hand, Boston has also had her famed treasure hunters.

Captain Thomas Claymore of the Boston-built *Trial,* using a diving tub, reaped a respectable fortune from a sunken Spanish ship that had sailed the Caribbean. Governor Winthrop launched one of several matrimonial ventures with the captain's well-heeled widow.

Sir William Phips was the most prominent Boston adventurer. In 1687, Phips, with logistical support from the British crown, raised tons of silver and gold from the Bahamas wreck of the galleon *Concepcion.* One sour note in the salvage account is that Phips allegedly impressed Indian divers into service. The monarch was so elated over Phips's replenishing the royal coffers that he knighted him and appointed him Massachusetts governor. With his share of treasure the new governor could well afford to keep his mind on affairs of state. A shipmaster friend of Phips is said to have gone raving mad over his cut of the good fortune, so that paradoxically for this poor soul, it was bad fortune indeed.

Following Phips's demise, his residence was reportedly owned by a controversial Captain Gruchy, a freelancer, who in the 1740s war between England and France captured many French ships. The prize vessels were taken to Boston for auctioning, and Gruchy sank two or three to form a wharf at his house. He then constructed a secret subterranean passage from dwelling to shore. When the moon was hidden by a curtain of dark clouds over the bay, his booty-gorged ships were unloaded at high tide into boats with muffled oarlocks that pulled into the tunnel. The opening was cleverly disguised by the sunken hulks that formed Gruchy's wharf. Trusted sailors, guided by torchlight, strained under the contraband as they carried it up to the residence, cheating the authorities out of the king's share. The captain, like a seagoing Robin Hood, donated a set of magnificent chandeliers that had been destined for a French cathedral to one of Boston's most venerated churches. The difference between privateering under a letter of marque and piracy under the skull-and-crossbones flag was nearly invisible.

Storytellers following nebulous treasure accounts write about old Spanish warships wrecked near the harbor; however, these reports are officially refuted in a letter to the author from the Spanish government's Archivo Histórico Madrid Nacional. Adventuresome minds can transform lead ballast into silver ingots.

One mythical treasure is claimed to have been Philadelphia-minted 1804 silver dollars aboard a vessel that sank off the harbor entrance; the numismatic value at current prices would be millions of dollars. Neither the U.S. Department of the Treasury nor the National Archives, however, has any record of such a consignment to Boston, or of an associated loss during that period.

On the other hand, Boston Custom House books record that bullion and specie (coin) imported and exported between 1828 and 1847 totaled $46,314, 397 and $32,998,839, respectively. Might some of those shipments repose in strongboxes inside an offshore hulk? In fact, a number of vessels with consignments of specie were wrecked. A hull that split apart, though, might disperse booty or other cargo over great expanses of sea floor.

In research on shipwrecks, and even during the actual search, conjectures and errors have a way of insinuating themselves into factual context.

WARNING A VESSEL AWAY FROM SHORE.

Harbor Phenomena

Satan is supposed to have helped nearly sink a vessel in the harbor. Shortly after colonial officials hanged Thomas Jones's spouse for alleged witchcraft, Jones went aboard the anchored *Welcome* for travel to more hospitable lands. A dusty reference work states that "the weather was calm, yet the ship fell to rolling, and so deep it was feared she would founder. Great weight was placed on one side to trim her, and she would heel over to the other side. The County Court was then in session, and, upon hearing that the husband of the executed witch was on board, sent officers to arrest him. No sooner was the warrant shown than the rolling of the ship began to stop, and after the man was in prison it moved no more." It has also been determined, however, that the *Welcome* had a substantial number of horses as cargo, and one may wonder if their weight, movement, and positioning could have affected the vessel's stability.

Extraordinary happenings at sea are plentiful, particularly in disasters. *The Boston Globe* of May 2, 1960, ran an article titled *Mystery Vessel Sinks off Boston After Single SOS*. It disclosed: "The only clue found near the point where the vessel went down was a blue-gray fedora hat, which the Coast Guard said had apparently not been long in the water." The distress call was no hoax, for a helicopter crew had glimpsed the bottom of a long black hull, just before it sank from view. The story might be straight from the Bermuda Triangle.

Over the centuries, corroborative accounts appeared about a sixty-foot sea serpent, a devilish "finny" creature capable of wrecking a vessel. First sighted in Massachusetts Bay in 1638, it appeared off Boston Harbor in the early 1800s. An authoritative reference work speaks of "a sea serpent or snake that lay coiled up like a cable upon a rock at Cape Ann. A boat passing by it with English aboard and two Indians would have shot the serpent, but the Indians dissuaded them, saying if he were not killed outright, they would be in danger of their lives."

An antiquarian in a later period quipped, "The stuffed skin of the monster would never be destined to adorn the walls of any museum, or his remains repose in any pickle other than the native brine of the titan of the deep."

Apparently other mysteries troubled these waters, including a report in the *Boston Traveler* of September 7, 1935:

> *A huge sea mammal, 25 feet long and weighing 5 tons, which has the body of a whale and the head of a blackfish, but is neither, is stranded on the shore off Point Allerton Road, Allerton.*
>
> *Veterans of the deep scratched their heads and wrinkled their brows as they gazed upon the strange mammal which was previously seen moving about between Boston Light and Point Allerton. Only a few days ago a whale landed on the beach nearby. The whale was 38 feet long and weighed 10 tons.*
>
> *Members of the Point Allerton Lifesaving Station ventured to guess that the strange mammal might have been searching for the whale and become lost. At any rate, it rested on the sand and attracted crowds.*

Boston Harbor had a *Jaws* episode on August 11, 1936. The *Boston Post* described the frightening incident:

> *Men with hunting rifles drove off a sea monster, identified by all who saw it as a man-eating shark, after it had terrorized hundreds of bathers in the Weymouth section of Fore River for more than an hour last night. The shark brought his surprise raid to a grim climax when he started to attack eight children marooned on a raft off Sandy Beach, Weymouth.*
>
> *The monster is believed to have measured 15 feet in length. While the children screamed with terror, the dorsal fin of the sea monster moved slowly back and forth between raft and shore. Whether he would have eventually tried to snatch the children from the raft is not known, for about that time Herbert Crawford of 37 Wachusetts Road, North Weymouth, with his brother John, came to the rescue, armed with rifles, in a boat equipped with an outboard motor.*
>
> *Crawford chased the shark almost to the Fore River bridge before he caught up with him. He fired a shot at close range and the shark dove and came up some 20 feet away. Then with a swirl of his tail and a stream of reddish bubbles in his wake, the fish disappeared and was not seen again.*

The Weymouth incident occurred a couple of weeks after a Dorchester youth lost his life in a shark attack near the Cape Cod Canal. Could the shark observed at Weymouth have been the Cape man-eater? Was this a classic rogue shark on the prowl? It might surprise even an astute marine science researcher to realize how many great white sharks make an appearance along the Massachusetts coastline.

Boston Custom House following a gale

Historical Flotsam and Jetsam

The *New Englands Prospect,* printed in 1633, described Boston Harbor as "made by a great company of islands, in which there is room for the anchorage of 500 ships."

Massachusetts boasted in 1676 that 730 craft of various tonnages were sailing from the Boston area.

In the summer of 1711, Admiral Hovenden Walker arrived at Boston with the largest fleet that had ever floated at one time upon its waters. The armada, which was to attack the French, included fifteen men-o'-war and forty transports, upon which Massachusetts troops embarked to swell the British regiments. The expedition, however, was devastated at the mouth of the St. Lawrence, not by the French garrison, but by a great gale in which nine ships, along with about 900 men, went to the bottom.

An English fleet provoked colonists in November 1747, after a number of tars (sailors) deserted men-o'-war at anchor in the harbor. To replace them, Commodore Knowles ordered press gangs to forcibly enlist sailors from colonial merchant ships, even to take citizens from Boston streets. The town soon seethed in protest, armed crowds assembled, a vessel was burned, and British naval officers were seized as hostages. Release of the kidnapped Bostonians was demanded, but Knowles, outraged by this insurrection against the king's officers, threatened to bombard Boston. Fortunately, reason prevailed, and when the fleet finally sailed for England, "there was not a Boston boy on board."

Historian William Cullen Bryant wrote that the spirited citizenry "had not been moved in the least by a threat to knock their town about their ears, and abated nothing of their assertion of the sacredness of personal liberty."

A mercantile reference work shows that 567 vessels cleared the port of

Boston between December 21, 1767, and December 31, 1768, bound for these places:

London – 43	Europe – 1
Liverpool – 5	Gibraltar – 5
Glasgow – 6	Newfoundland – 42
Bristol – 2	Quebec – 8
Great Britain – 9	Nova Scotia – 48
Ireland – 4	Honduras – 1
Spain and Portugal – 10	West Indies – 137
Western Islands – 3	East Coast locations – 243

A particularly disastrous tempest erupted in Massachusetts waters on October 20, 1770, destroying more than 100 vessels and an equal number of lives. Only one ship rode out the gale while anchored in Nantasket Roads. Fifteen craft were cast ashore on harbor islands, but few were extensively damaged.

For all their tiers of cannon, even formidable warships were almost powerless against the harbor elements. Fitz-Henry Smith, Jr., a renowned author, read before the Bostonian Society that "The storm of November 2, 1778, gave d'Estaing [French naval commander] the opportunity to escape the British, but the departure of the French fleet was not uneventful. The ill-fated *Zèle* (74 guns), grounded hard, and the *Protecteur* (74 guns) and flagship *Languedoc* (80 guns) behaved so badly with their new masts that it was feared they would be wrecked."

D'Estaing wrote that the flagship was never in greater danger. She would not steer, and "an irresistible current pushed her ashore." Only by immediately anchoring did the crew save the vessel. One familiar with the tides at Hull can easily believe the admiral's story. A young officer, Pléville LePeley, captain of the *Languedoc,* had his right leg carried away by a cannon ball. The wooden edition replacing it was twice shot off in his later years.

Winter gales sometimes cast ashore mementos from nameless hulks. Many of the nautical items used for the art of war—or peace—can endure oxidation and abrasion in the depths for centuries. An unusual antique grappled up in Nantasket Roads many years ago was an immense anchor. It had a wooden stock, 20-foot shank, 28-inch ring, 6 1/2-foot flukes, and weighed almost 8,000 pounds. Local inhabitants claimed that the anchor was lost by the French warship *Poictiers,* assigned to protecting the harbor entrance during the Revolutionary War.

During 1790 a traveler wrote, "The Bay of Boston is spacious enough to contain in a manner the Navy of England. The masts of ships here at proper seasons of the year make a kind of wood of trees." A 1794 visitor commented, "The harbor of Boston is of this date crowded with vessels. Eighty-four sails have been counted lying at two of the wharfs only. It is reckoned that not less than four hundred and fifty ships, brigs, schooners, sloops, and other small craft are now in this port."

Furthermore, a 1794 description of Boston in Massachusetts Historical Society collections reveals:

> *There are eighty wharves and quays, chiefly on the east side of the town. Of these the most distinguished is Boston Pier, or Long Wharf, which extends from the bottom of State Street, one thousand seven hundred and forty-three feet into the harbor; the breadth is one hundred and four feet, at the end are seventeen feet at low water. Adjoining this wharf, to the north of it, and near the center, is a convenient quay called Minot's T, from the name of its former proprietor, and the form of it resembling that letter.*

The early to middle years of the nineteenth century flooded Boston's shipping enterprises with wealth, from California gold-rush clippers to packets on the Baltic run, and East Indiamen of the China trade. The latter voyages at times even traded in opium. A typical display was a lump of gold weighing fifteen pounds, brought back from the West Coast and proudly shown in a Boston merchant's window. Massachusetts fortunes rose and fell on the tide of ocean commerce. The waterfront pulsed with activity, and gabled brick and Quincy granite warehouses bulged with merchandise destined for all parts. Boston docks were chafed by topsail schooners, brigantines, and tall-masted barks.

Arrivals and clearances at Boston, excepting British mail steamers, from January 1, 1840, to December 31, 1845, recorded 28,821 and 16,335 vessels, respectively. Many craft sailing under coasting licenses cleared at the Custom House only when transporting debentured goods (goods on which a duty is paid); thus, the arrivals significantly exceeded clearances. During these five years, 5,503 foreign vessels used the port:

British – 5,360	Russian – 5	German – 2
Swedish – 37	Austrian – 3	Belgian – 1
Sicilian – 31	Dutch – 3	Portuguese – 1
Danish – 10	Sardinian – 3	Bremen – 6
Hamburg – 10	Spanish – 3	Norwegian – 6
Prussian – 10	Venezuelan – 3	French – 5

Some of America's most illustrious craft left the Hub of the Universe in triumph, only to founder eventually, many of them off a desolate shore.

Donald McKay of East Boston, the so-called Leonardo da Vinci of shipbuilding, set the stage for a glorious era.

His great *Flying Cloud,* launched in 1851, stranded on the New Brunswick coast during 1874, and was refloated in badly strained condition. While undergoing repairs she was damaged by accidental fire and was broken up for her metal. The largest wooden ship ever constructed, McKay's 4,555-ton *Great Republic,* fell to a watery grave off Bermuda in 1872 when a hurricane proved too much for an aging hull. The southern side of Boston Harbor also had its artisans, such as Herbert N. Keen, who in 1878 crafted the Weymouth-built *Alice Knowles,* a famous whaler that was lost at sea. Another beautiful creation was the titanic seven-masted *Thomas W. Lawson,* designed by B. B. Crowninshield and assembled at Bethlehem Ship Yard in Quincy. The largest schooner ever sent down the ways, this steel 5,200-ton behemoth sank off the Scilly Islands near the English Channel, primarily because of improper ballasting. A superstitious Boston salt observed that the vessel had thirteen letters in her name and went down on Friday, December 13, 1907.

Shipwreck losses were so frequent at times during the heyday of sail that some marine insurance firms had to get out of the underwriting business. Insurance companies would vigorously battle claimants by countering

Launch of the Flying Cloud *at East Boston*

that too few anchor cables were out, anchors were too small, or seamanship was questionable.

An appalling 458 American vessels were listed as lost and missing for 1836: 11 steamers, 144 ships, 60 barks, 80 brigs, 160 schooners, and 3 sloops.

A report of the period chastised the system for manning ships with "worthless, drunken, inefficient men, scraped out of the dens and purlieus of our great cities, and rushed out into the ocean, and flung to the winds…" In 1848, a meeting of the Board of Underwriters, who were the presidents of all the Boston marine insurance companies, prepared a public notice:

> *That this Board will hereafter examine into all cases of shipwreck or disaster, happening without extraordinary cause, to vessels insured by any of their respective companies; and ascertain if the cause or causes of such shipwreck or disaster are to be attributed to the carelessness, want of proper judgment, neglect, or the important precaution of trying the soundings on approaching the land, or any other gross negligence on the part of the master or other navigator of such vessel or vessels.*

At times the underwriters could be downright stingy, as when it was alleged that Mr. Tower, the wreckmaster,

> *left Hull at 4 o'clock, P.M. in the midst of a driving N.E. storm, the snow a foot and a half deep, and travelled horseback to Boston to give information that the ship* Lapland *from Liverpool, with a valuable cargo, was ashore upon Long Beach. His mission was successful; the tug-steamer* Robert B. Forbes *went down and saved the ship and cargo, the crew and passengers. Mr. Tower reached home again at 2 o'clock the next morning, having been on horseback about eight hours. The underwriters paid him for his valuable and commendable services only sixteen dollars, one-half of which he had to pay on the road for extra horses. Mean enough!*

A Tongue-in-Cheek Meeting
on Wrecks

Wrecks were so directly interwoven with Hull residents' daily lives that they could bring levity to this normally serious subject. Granted, the townsfolk, especially the wreckers, were not unduly upset by a well-laden ship run aground, as its salvage could help stock winter larders and provide "ballast" to empty pockets. Moreover, townsfolk derived personal pride from rescuing mariners in distress. Yet the frequency of such wrecks and the resulting litter-strewn shoreline could become a nuisance because they demanded the residents' valuable time. Consequently, a public meeting was held in 1848 on the subject of marine disasters. *Notes on the Sea Shore*, a report of that meeting published by the "Shade of Alden," contains this tongue-in-cheek resolution drafted by those in attendance:

> *WHEREAS, the quiet, industrious citizens of Hull have noticed, with regret and indignation, but with the feelings of men and of christians, as they humbly trust, the rapid increase of shipwrecks, and of accidents to our mercantile marine, on Nantasket Beach, the Hardings, Cohasset rocks, at Marshfield, Scituate, and other places in the vicinity: And whereas, those which have occurred of late are believed to have been caused, for the most part, through the ignorance, inexperience, carelessness, or want of proper attention and skill on the part of those in command of the vessels which have been partially or wholly wrecked—in some instances involving the loss of valuable human lives as well as property: And whereas, of late years, we have been shocked at the frequent midnight calls made upon us to proceed to Long Beach and its neighborhood, to save the fragments of wrecks and the lives of mariners: And whereas, there is reason to believe that*

Old representation of Boston Lighthouse

many of the youthful captains sailing out of Boston are unfitted for the business they are engaged in, either from a want of experience as seamen, sound judgment and skill as navigators, or the absence of a proper alacrity when approaching the coast, and who are too often put in command of vessels through the undue influence of wealthy relatives: And whereas, these things are becoming highly offensive to the unpretending, hard-fisted citizens of Hull and of Hingham, some of whom have followed fishing twenty-five and thirty years, without running ashore or without meeting with a single accident: Therefore,

Resolved, That there are four points to the compass—N. E. S. W.; and any captain of a vessel who cannot box the compass, deserves to have his ears boxed.

Resolved, That an education received by rubbing against the walls of a college, or passing through its halls, is not so serviceable to a sea captain as one received upon the Ocean, amidst high winds, heavy seas, and hard knocks.

Resolved, That maps and charts are useful to navigators at sea, and he who neglects to study them thoroughly is a blockhead of the first class, and ought not to be entrusted with the command of a first class ship.

Resolved, That the beach at Marshfield is not Boston Light House, "any way you can fix it."

Resolved, That no captain of a ship has a right to run his jib-boom into the lantern of Boston Light, through mistake or careless-ness—supposing himself to be fifty miles from the shore at the time.

Resolved, That the light on Eastern Point, at the entrance of Gloucester Harbor, a steady light, cannot well be mistaken, except through sheer ignorance, for that at the entrance of Boston Harbor, which is a revolving one.

Resolved, That Boston Light and Cape Ann are thirty miles apart, and cannot be made much shorter, even by the aid of a straight railroad from point to point.

Resolved, That Cohasset rocks, on the South shore, although they resemble some others, on the North shore, are not one and the same thing; and it is important that this fact should be generally understood.

Resolved, That any captain, while nearing the rocks spoken of, or any others, who fails to use his deep-sea line, or his hand-lead, constantly, until he finds out his right position, is unfit to have charge of a valuable ship and cargo, and the more valuable lives of her crew and passengers; his own is of but little consequence to the rising generation.

Resolved, As the deliberate opinion of this meeting, that when a sea captain, if approaching our coast, his course due W., finds him-self getting rapidly into shoal water, the safest way is to wear ship, and run to the Eastward, instead of running plump upon the beach or the rocks.

Resolved, That a sea captain might as well be a hard-drinker, at once, as to be extremely ignorant of his reckoning and his bearings, under a bright sky and a brighter sun.

Resolved, That our labors as wreckers are often severe and per-ilous, but well-intended, disinterested, and zealous; and that we look to the underwriters for a proper remuneration, in all cases where assistance is rendered to vessels in distress. It is not right for them to cavil at small charges, when they are just.

Resolved, That Father Bates be respectfully requested to preach a sermon upon the important points embraced in these resolutions.

At the suggestion of the chairman, the following resolution was added to those reported by the committee:

Resolved, That any captain who runs his vessel ashore, from inadvertence or other cause, and throws only half his cargo over-board, where it can be fished up with facility by wreckers, is entitled to more consideration and favor, at the hands of underwriters, than he who meets with a total loss, vessel and cargo.

U.S. Life Saving Service exhibit of surfboats and other equipment
(Courtesy: Society for the Preservation of New England Antiquities)

Samaritans of the Coast

—⌇—

Bay State waters, including Boston Harbor, are strewn with rotting timbers and rusting hull plates from several thousand hulks, silent evidence not merely of human ineptitude but nature's harshness.

Most perils that rob people of their lives strike without warning. The shipwreck victim, however, undergoes special agony. He observes mountainous waves rising toward a threatening sky, black clouds scudding past, and a more-or-less indistinguishable line of coast. In stormy weather with an onshore wind, the sailor fears nothing so much as nearby land. Further imagine the shrill wind, sharp enough to cut sails to ribbons. The ship, with resounding groans, grates against a ledge, perhaps briefly pulling free. At last the vessel, rolling and pitching, is forced against the shore—but still the victim remains in suspense. A mast snaps like a pipestem, and an avalanche of water shatters the ship's boat. Previous dread gives way to the terror of doom.

In Edgar Allan Poe's *The Pit and the Pendulum,* the victim knows that with destruction inevitably descending upon him, life will be forfeited. A shipwreck, however, holds just enough hope to heighten such slow torture. The shipwrecked mariner could sight a lantern or flare held by the watchful patrol from a lifesaving station.

During early maritime trade the government was generally tardy in lighting ominous coastal points and marking treacherous areas. Few lighthouses were built, and mariners long depended upon charts and navigational directions prepared much earlier by foreign visitors. Frequent wrecks and losses of life finally shocked bureaucrats into adopting definite provisions for protecting commerce.

The United States Coast Survey, organized in 1832, initiated accurate and detailed study of our shores. In 1852, an efficient U.S. Lighthouse Board was established. Lighthouses already erected were improved and fitted with advanced light-concentrating lenses. Along with new lighthouses and lightships, these innovations enhanced navigation and decreased the hazards in travel on the sea. Little was done, though, to aid passengers and crews on vessels already wrecked. The government took steps in the right direction and, where possible, ordered U.S. Navy ships to patrol shore waters during the severest seasons. But the naval vessels' size and draft made them helpless in shoal waters, and so they were replaced on patrol duties by U.S. Revenue Marine craft. Though limited, these operations rescued hundreds from the sea.

Timely and effective aid to the shipwrecked, however, required establishing lifesaving stations all along the American coastline, but the necessary national organization was not formed until years later.

In the meantime, the Massachusetts Humane Society was actively performing voluntary lifesaving work on Bay State shores. Founded in 1785, the society in 1791 erected the first refuge hut on Lovell's Island to help the shipwrecked. Additional huts were built at strategic locations. A lifeboat station was constructed at nearby Cohasset in 1807, and the number of stations was increased to cover Boston Harbor and elsewhere.

Massachusetts Humane Society surfboats were double-ended, of the best material available, and as light in weight as safety permitted. These boats were wide, with ends not too sharp so that waves would lift them easily during launching. Cork bumper-cushions were secured below the gunwales for flotation and at times also along the bilge under the thwarts. With these and the air tanks sometimes added inside, the craft would still

Surfboat Nantasket *and Hull Volunteers* (**Courtesy: The Means Library, Hull**)

support the occupants even when swamped. They were rowed single- or double-banked and steered with a long oar like the typical whaleboat. The legendary surfboat *Nantasket* safely bore her crews on many harrowing rescues.

The society used the Hunt gun and projectile for firing lines to stranded vessels. Invented by Edmund S. Hunt of Weymouth, Massachusetts, this ordnance was simple to operate, light, and dependable, when properly handled. The gun, charge, projectile, and line were all the crew needed to reach a ship from shore.

Subsequently, enough lifesaving stations were added to provide quick rescue response all along Massachusetts shores. Nantasket Beach, though, was one of the society's toughest assignments, for wrecks occurred nearly everywhere along its shore. Most of the organization's records on disasters were burned in the Great Boston Fire of 1872.

Captain Joshua James of Hull, most illustrious member of the society (and later the U.S. Life Saving Service), devoted sixty years to furnishing aid to shipwrecked mariners. His many decorations for unselfish devotion to duty included a gold medal presented by act of the U.S. Congress, for unparalleled lifesaving accomplishments. Captain James, highly esteemed by his crews, warned them before one rescue mission that the chances of returning looked dim, the surf was so violent. When the captain asked for volunteers, every man offered himself without hesitation. A chapter in lifesaving history came to an end in 1902, when Captain James, then age 75, ordered a routine boat drill. Upon landing after the exercise, he turned to the crew and remarked, "The tide is ebbing." He then died and fell to the beach.

The Boston Marine Society, incorporated in 1754, over the years has recommended many safeguards against shipwrecks. Samuel G. Drake, in his *History and Antiquities of Boston,* explained that the society consisted of "a considerable number

Captain Joshua James, America's most famous lifesaver—and one of the many heroes of Hull
(Courtesy: U.S. Coast Guard)

U.S. Life Saving Service Crew with Captain Joshua James, Hull, Mass., 1893. Photograph by Baldwin Coolidge. **(Courtesy: Society for the Preservation of New England Antiquities)**

Funeral cortege of Captain Joshua James **(Courtesy: U.S. Coast Guard)**

U.S. Life Saving Service crew and surfboat Point Allerton, *at Hull, Mass., 1893. Photograph by Baldwin Coolidge.* **(Courtesy: Society for the Preservation of New England Antiquities)**

of persons who were or had been masters of ships or other vessels. They associated to improve the knowledge of the coast by communicating their observations, inward and outward, of the variations of the needle, the sounding, courses, and distances, and all other remarkable things about it in writing, to be lodged with the Society, for the making of navigation more safe."

Paradoxically, when the War of 1812 threatened Boston's security, the organization recommended sinking hulks in strategic channels. Vessels were to be specifically fitted so that they could be expeditiously raised after hostilities ceased. The society has been responsible for appointing Boston's pilot commissioners, who, in turn, select harbor pilots. In sailing days these mariners would fight through great rolling swells to reach a vessel's towering side, climb the whiplashing Jacob's ladder, and navigate her in to port.

The United States considered methods for aiding wrecked vessels, proposing a limited number of lifesaving stations along the more dangerous parts of the Atlantic Coast, but excluded Massachusetts. Manning these stations saved many persons and recovered much property. At times, however, the stations and equipment fell into disrepair.

Before 1871, the government supplied lifeboats to town corporations and benevolent societies, to help them supplement official lifesaving activities. Some of these boats not only were not kept in shape, but one in particular was employed as a trough for mixing concrete. A more extensive lifesaving system was vigorously acted upon in 1871 to combat the threat to

Equipment of
Massachusetts Humane Society Stations

LIFE-BOAT AND EQUIPMENT

1. Life-Boat (size and model to suit location).
2. Boat Carriage and Tackle (where necessary).
3. Oars, a set of the best ash. A spare oar for each two the boat pulls.
4. Steering Oars (two).
5. Boat-Hooks (two).
6. Cork Life-Jackets for each of the crew.
7. Anchor.
8. Cable, 60 fathoms best 2-inch Manila.
9. Small Hand Grapnel and Heaving Stick, line of 1-inch Manilla.
10. One Sharp Axe, secured under the main thwart.
11. Lantern.

GUN CART AND EQUIPMENT

1. Gun Cart.
2. Hunt Gun.
3. Six Life-Saving Projectiles.
4. Six Reels or Cans of Shot Line.
5. Whip Line (600 Fathoms), 1 1/4-inch best quality Manila.
6. Tally Boards (French and English).
7. Hawser (300 fathoms), 3-inch best quality Manila.
8. Breeches-Buoy (cork).
9. Sand Anchor or Iron Stake with Pennant.
10. Tackle (two double tail-blocks, with 2-inch fall).
11. Crotch (wood).
12. Lantern.
13. Magazine (copper).
14. Powder (twenty charges of 4 ozs.).
15. Primers (one box) with Laniard.
16. Cart Cover.
17. Axe.
18. Shovel and Pick.
19. Night Signals (one dozen).
20. Brass Spool for attaching Hawser to Whip-Line.

our expanding commerce. During 1872, the first of a number of lifesaving stations was established on Cape Cod.

The U.S. Life Saving Service was approved as a separate organization by Congress in 1878. Each lifesaving station was controlled by a keeper, who was selected with great care. He must be of unquestionable character, good habits, mentally and physically sound, and exceptionally knowledgeable about boat handling. Determined efforts were made to eliminate political, social, or personal influences. Keepers selected lifesaving crews from seamen living near the station. Rigorously tested by a government physician and then for ability with small boats and ways of the sea, the crews' courageous motto was, "You have to go out, but you don't have to come back."

The crews, commonly called surfmen, lived at the stations during the active season, when wrecks usually occurred. Normally, most stations had

The breeches buoy was vital in rescue operations at marine disasters.

at least one large boat of six oars, and therefore six men made up the regular complement. During the roughest part of the wreck season, a seventh surfman was added to help launch and beach in heavy seas and to keep the station prepared for receiving survivors and fellow surfmen after a disaster.

Patrols reached as far as practicable along the coast in each direction from the station. The day watch was kept by a surfman in a lookout tower. For remote stretches, a beach patrol went out at reasonable intervals. On the night patrol of four watches, two surfmen set out in opposite directions along the beach as far as the station boundaries. Often they had to battle surging tides, excruciating cold, cutting wind, and stinging sand. Patrolmen approaching an adjacent station continued along the beach until they met the patrol from that station.

The patrolmen were equipped with lanterns and signal flares and were familiar with the International Code flag system. Once they found a vessel in distress or a wreck, they lit the flares, warning vessels in precarious waters, or signaling shipwrecked mariners that their plight was noticed and help was coming.

Masters were particularly cautioned that if they should be driven ashore anywhere near a station, they must remain on board until assistance arrived. They should not attempt to land through surf in their own boats until the last hope of help had vanished. (Often, when the sea is comparatively smooth, a dangerous but unseen surf is running several hundred yards offshore. From a vessel the surf never looks as violent as it actually is.) Many lives were lost unnecessarily when crews of stranded vessels, thus deceived, attempted to land in the ship's boats.

The Massachusetts Humane Society and the U.S. Life Saving Service are indeed proud chapters in our maritime history. Since 1915 their descendant, the U.S. Coast Guard, has filled many more illustrious pages, with deepwater action on the world's oceans to rescues in Boston Harbor.

Breeches-buoy apparatus in operation

Catastrophic
Nineteenth-Century Storms

⚯

During the triple tempest in December 1839, ninety vessels and approximately 200 seamen succumbed along the Massachusetts coastline. The *Gloucester Telegram* commented: "The storm king it would seem had urged the elements to do their worst, while he himself appeared to ride on the whirlwind and direct the havoc and devastation that were committed around us."

During these gales Henry Wadsworth Longfellow immortalized the "Wreck of the Hesperus." Although the tragedy he referred to took place at Norman's Woe, a reef on the North Shore, a schooner named *Hesperus* was damaged at Rowe's Wharf in Boston. Longfellow may have found the name *Hesperus* more romantic to set to poetry than that of the actual Norman's Woe wreck; however, this is a matter of dispute.

On April 14–16, 1851, the tragic Minot's Light gale toppled the famed lighthouse off nearby Cohasset into the sea as its keepers perished in mountainous waves. Damage to shipping in Boston Harbor was relatively light: only two strandings were recorded. The abnormally high tide, which crested at a record 15.62 feet, was destructive to property along the waterfront, and State Street could be negotiated only by boat.

About the Great Storm on November 25–26, 1888, the *Boston Journal* lamented:

> All day yesterday reports poured into this City of wrecks all along the coast as the result of the severe gale. An unprecedented number of vessels—estimated as high as 40—were cast ashore all round Massachusetts Bay (several disasters in Boston Harbor). Some of them were total wrecks, but the saddest feature was the loss of life. One

Destruction of original Minot's Ledge Lighthouse; although off Cohasset, it is traditionally associated with Boston Harbor.

fishing schooner with fifteen men went down and carried all but one. Another schooner lost three men, and another had two officers washed overboard. Besides these known cases of death, there are grave suspicions that other crews have been swallowed up by the waves. Abandoned vessels have been found, but their crews have not been heard from.

The *Gloucester Times* told a sad tale about the wreck of the *Bertha F. Walker* in Boston Harbor. The captain, a hefty man, spurned his crew's pleading to join them in the rigging, instead deciding to chance the deck. Upon hearing his commander's refusal the mate, who was high in a safe place, descended to join the captain and declined to leave his side. Just as the two men were heading toward the forecastle, a towering wave struck the schooner, sweeping both to their deaths.

A further report in the *Gloucester Times* disclosed: "Nantasket Beach is lined with wrecks, and wreckage from vessels which must have gone down in the Bay has strewn the beach from Point Allerton to Atlantic Hill."

According to Judeth Van Hamm, Director, Hull Lifesaving Museum, the bemedaled Massachusetts Humane Society volunteers rescued twenty-nine mariners, including one overeager salvager, from several vessels within thirty-six hours.

This is the gale in which the surfboat *Nantasket* gained everlasting fame. Built for the Humane Society from a design by Captain Samuel James of Hull, and commanded by Captain Joshua James, it was responsible for many rescues.

The *Boston Daily Globe* emphasized in later years that "Capt. Samuel James, her designer, like his brother Joshua, is a famous lifesaver. He has received no remuneration for his invention; the fact that he has been instrumental in saving a multitude of lives seems to be the only satisfaction he desires. It is estimated that these two brothers have saved more lives from the sea than any two men living in the world."

The newspapers expressed amazement about the brig *Alice*, one exposé reading: "Almost as soon as she struck, the wreckers began their work, and it had been remarkable to see the manner in which she had been broken up and carried away. Every spar and every inch of rigging has been cut away and carried off, together with her cargo, and nothing now remains but her hulk. If the keelson remains another 24 hours, it will be considered something phenomenal."

Distress guns boomed aboard drifting vessels during the February 1, 1898, snowstorm, which beset the coast with gale-force winds and fifteen inches of snow. The two-masted lumber schooner *Clara Jane*, blown across Massachusetts Bay from Magnolia, slipped through the outer gauntlet of ledges and fetched up on Great Brewster Island without even an evident leak. Several ships were stranded around the inner harbor.

Another howler was the awesome Portland Gale of November 26–27, 1898, in which wind velocity reached about 100 miles an hour. Almost 150 wrecks littered the coast, and around 455 lives were lost. The storm had no parallel in marine annals. On the ill-fated 280-foot *Portland*, which had steamed from Boston Harbor, 175 passengers and crew members became victims in Massachusetts Bay. Not even one survivor would tell of the steamer's end.

The *Quincy Daily Ledger* lead caption read: "Massachusetts Bay One Vast Mass of Wreckage—Many Sailors Went to Bottom with Vessels." The writer related a melancholy tragedy:

> *A bit of bamboo, which was picked up in the surf, brought a story of death and the loss of a schooner. The fragment was found tossing about in the waves, and it contained a letter. The message was as follows: "We will be lost—13 of us—in the fishing schooner* White Wings *of Gloucester. Have no bottle to put it in. Everything is gone. We are about to go on a raft. Henry Wilder and Frank Haskins are dead. If I could only see my wife and darling child again. Signed Albert Simmons."*

A more fortunate incident closed the episode when the 974-ton coasting steamer *John J. Hill* was forced toward shore at the National Sailor's Home near Merrymount, Quincy. The captain lashed himself to the bridge and stood doggedly at the wheel until she grounded. When at last convinced his craft would not break up, the skipper attempted to leave the bridge but found himself frozen fast to the deck. Crew members released the captain from his post by hacking away with an axe.

A writer for *Harper's Monthly Magazine* reported:

I never pass the Light [Boston Lighthouse] without seeing again in the uncertain dawn of a biting November morning six poor sailors frozen in the rigging of a wrecked schooner, like six long lumps of ice. The comfort of the Light-keeper's home was only a few hundred feet from them as their souls went out; had it been miles away, the case would have been no more hopeless on that awful night of the great gale of November 27, 1898. It was in this gale the steamer Portland *foundered in the bay, with never a soul near two hundred on board spared to tell of her end. On the morning following the gale—they now call it "The Portland Gale" on all that coast—I counted fifty-five wrecks on the shores of Boston Harbor.*

Salvage Tricks of the Trade

Salvagers such as the Boston Wrecking Company were established in most major ports in the mid to late 1800s. Staunch steamers were fitted with expensive diving equipment, tackle, pontoons, and pumps to refloat sunken or stranded vessels. Wreckers with less capital, such as those from the town of Hull, equipped small coasting schooners with simpler devices rather than costly gear, such as wooden casks strung together.

An old-time salvage expert, Captain Howard Patterson, explains in an article in the turn-of-the-century *Sailor's Magazine and Seamen's Friend* that when a vessel sinks in a harbor, or in sheltered waters, raising her is a comparatively simple piece of work, no matter how deep the water. But in exposed waters, shallow though they may be, success is extremely doubtful, for the surge or heaving of the sea is apt to tear the pontoons and massive cable apart.

Strange as it may appear, it is generally easier to raise a vessel from the bottom in a deep harbor than to save a ship stranded on the beach, even if her hull has sustained no damage. Often the salvors must wait for a strong storm to pile waves high up on the beach before they get water enough to buoy up the hulk.

When their task is pulling a small stranded ship off the shore, the wrecking tug carries anchors seaward with hawsers attached. Dropping the anchors, they send the long rope cables to the wreck, where they are rigged around capstans or windlasses to bring a strain upon them. The tugs send the ends of other hawsers to the vessel, and when everything is ready the powerful tugs point their bows seaward and the engines are driven ahead at full speed, while the men on board the wreck revolve the windlasses to pull on the lines connected to the anchors.

When a vessel goes on the beach "light"—with little cargo or ballast— she will naturally be thrown higher on the sand than a ship deeply loaded, and floating her is much harder, for after the storm is spent the waters recede and sometimes leave the light vessel high and dry. On the other hand, a deeply laden vessel will take to the bottom farther out, and removing her cargo will often make it possible to float her off with little trouble.

The hawsers employed in pulling a vessel off the beach varied from twelve to twenty inches thick and were about 1,200 feet long. The anchors weighed from two to three and a half tons.

When a large vessel is driven high up the beach, the heaviest anchors and thickest hawsers are used, but because the latter are too unwieldy and weighty to revolve around a capstan or windlass, they are rigged so that they will "go to the cables." Their ends are made fast on board, and with powerful tackles the hawsers are stretched until all possible tension is put on them.

When a heavy sea rolls around the stranded vessel and starts to float her, the strain upon the hawsers pulls her toward the sea, slackening the lines. The wreckers immediately take in the slack and wait for the next sea to help the cables drag the craft nearer deep water.

These are tough times for salvagers, for it takes unusual courage to face a gale on a windward shore, with a wrecked vessel under their feet, and to labor hour after hour with all their strength to pull the craft closer and closer to the onrushing, roaring mountains of water that burst like thunder around the hull.

A vessel that is to be lifted from the sea bottom requires many novel and complicated appliances, such as large floats with powerful engines and suction pumps rigged on the decks; hawsers thick as an ordinary man's waist; huge chain cables that look as though they might support the earth, but whose massive welded links have been known to part like paper under the strain put upon them. The unwieldy pontoons, of wood or iron, are towed into position and securely anchored. These are hollow watertight cylinders and can be filled with water, sunk to the required depth, and then pumped out through pipe leading from them to engines on the floats. The pontoon ranges from 50 to 100 feet long, 8 to 16 feet wide, and 5 to 10 feet deep. The larger pontoons can raise about 400 tons each, and the smaller, 200 tons.

The pontoons are arranged in pairs on each side of the wreck; then divers pass small chains, the "messengers," under the keel of the sunken craft. These enable larger cables to be hauled under. Then the heavy cables are shackled to the pontoons on either side. The pontoons having been filled to sink them to water level, all the slack on the cables is taken in, they are pumped out, and the hull is lifted several feet from the bottom. The vessel is then towed into shallower water until it grounds again; the lifting operation is repeated until the deck of the wreck is brought above water, when she is pumped out and floated by her own buoyancy.

Local wreckers could perform small miracles with a crowbar and grappling iron in wresting treasures—or life's necessities—from King Neptune's locker. A news article revealed that one successful Hullonian fished up thirty-four crates of copper and galvanized tin in three days. In this environment, British Admiralty law prevailed in defining "flotsam" as wreck goods found floating on the surface; "jetsam" as material heaved overboard from a vessel involved in disaster; "legan" as heavy items thrown over the side with a line and buoy attached to mark the site; and "derelicts" as vessels abandoned to the elements by their crews.

Coal Collier Edward Peirce *sunk off South Boston Flats* (**Courtesy: Boston Public Library Print Dept.**)

Historians of bygone days have customarily taken their readers on calm-water excursions from Boston's docks. On the outward journey, their descriptions would generally include stories of shipwrecks at random locations. Most disasters, however, occurred as vessels were entering the harbor during a gale. Therefore, we will start from the seaward side of the harbor perimeter and work our way inward.

In these condensed accounts of shipwrecks, to ensure ease and timeliness in referring to wrecks and to delineate patterns of concentration, the harbor is divided into three major and traditional sections (inward bound): (1) Harding's Ledge, Hull, and the Outer Islands; (2) the Middle Islands; and (3) Boston and the Inner Islands.

Shipwrecks that occurred in these sections are presented chronologically. For readers who may wish to refer to the entire record of disasters, it is listed chronologically in the Appendix beginning on page 150.

THE OUTER HARBOR

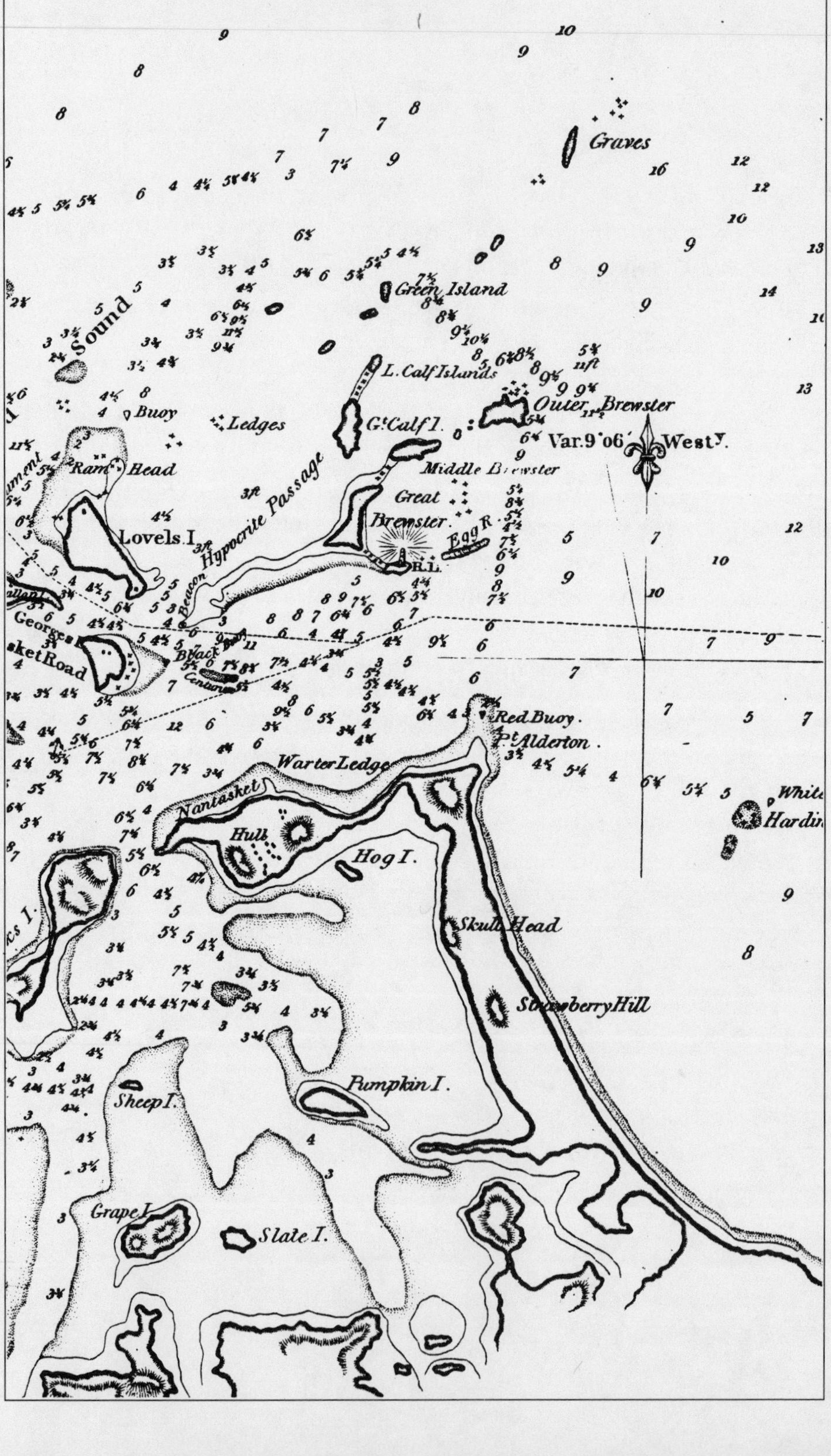

Graves

Green Island

L. Calf Islands

Outer Brewster

Var.9°06' West

G.t Calf I.

Middle Brewster

Ledges

Ram Head

Great Brewster

Egg R.

Hypocrite Passage

Lovels I.

Beacon

George's Road

Black

Red Buoy

P.t Alderton

Warter Ledge

Nantasket

Hull

Hog I.

White

Harding

Skull Head

Strawberry Hill

Pumpkin I.

Sheep I.

Grape I.

Slate I.

Sound

Buoy

The Outer Harbor

─◊◊◊─

Harding's Ledge Shipwrecks

Sailing from the Cape Cod vicinity, past the solitary sentry of Minot's Lighthouse off Cohasset, the first local threat we encounter is Harding's Ledge.
This shoal is Boston Harbor's rocky equivalent to the ill-reputed Isle of
Sable, which menaces ship traffic off Nova Scotia and is called the widow-
maker of the North Atlantic. Harding's Ledge, like the terrible hydra in
age-old fables, can lie partly submerged in the path of vessels to ensnare
mariners. When enveloped in haze, it is hardly distinguishable from the
brooding waves. Undoubtedly ships have been wrecked on Harding's
Ledge, but the sea has swallowed all traces. The extensive complex is eastward and about a mile and a half from Point Allerton. Boston Lighthouse
bears northwest roughly two and one-quarter miles. At low tide a large part
of Harding's is bare, with rocks awash. The ledge extends over an area of
about three-eighths of a square mile.

A Boston reporter of the period expressed the danger in this part of
the harbor:

> There were only two avenues to take when caught in a sudden snow-
> storm outside Boston Light, viz.: either run for the Light in the direc-
> tion last seen or round to, anchor, and cut away the masts. In either
> case the chances were fearfully small to escape destruction, for not one
> vessel in twenty would safely ride at her anchors outside Boston Light
> in a northeast gale, and there can hardly be one chance in ten of run-
> ning in for the Light in a snowstorm, unless the vessel is very near
> when the weather shuts in thick. The Harding's and Grave's Ledges
> have never been known to move out of the way of a vessel running
> such a fearful risk.

Minot's Ledge Lighthouse, off Cohasset, on the approach to Boston Harbor

During the 1800s, Harding's was marked with a wrought-iron beacon crowned with a horizontal cast-iron ring and attached wooden pendants. Three hundred and fifty yards east-northeast from the beacon, a black bell boat with a 500-pound bell was secured in seven and one-half fathoms. The so-called boat was ripped from her moorings in the January 1857 gale and thrown ashore on Nantasket Beach.

Ballou's Pictorial, a popular Boston paper, illustrated a bell boat on Harding's Ledge. The caption reads: "Built of boiler iron, hollow, with masts supporting a large and sonorous bell, with four clappers, so that it rings with the slightest motion of the wave or tide. The mast is about 15 feet in height, and the boat rigged with braces from the mast top to the stays, for shipwrecked persons to cling." Its warning peal also mournfully tolled for vessels claimed by the ledge. Indeed, the roll call of disasters is long.

Surf and Bell Boat, Harding's Ledge, Boston Harbor

PROVIDENCE - *Cannon Recovered by Divers*

With an incoming tide, rough seas, and thick weather, Harding's Ledge is almost invisible. These conditions could well have applied when the shipwreck generally considered the first to be officially recorded took place in the outer harbor. The brig *Providence,* Michael Gill commanding, struck the then unmarked ledge on September 28, 1697, while returning from Barbados, West Indies, with a cargo of rum. Despite the vessel's name, she was obviously unlucky, for this was her maiden voyage.

The *Providence* reportedly carried several pieces of armament for protection in foreign waters, and, in fact, a large iron cannon dating back to that era has been recovered by scuba divers. Fragments of several vessels are intermingled close to the ledge, swept there by swift tidal currents.

HOLLANDER - *Capsized with Cargo of Gin*

The brig *Hollander,* inward bound from Rotterdam, Holland, with a load of gin, linseed oil, and madder (a red dye root), capsized at Harding's Ledge on February 25, 1836. Owned by a Boston firm, she was ninety-five days out of the Dutch port. Ironically, the crew had been taken aboard the outgoing brig *Fame,* headed for Havana. The *Fame* did not put about back to Boston, however, and *Hollander* survivors made the trip to Cuba, returning to their original destination several months later. It appears that *Fame* was short of crew members and shanghaied the shipwrecked mariners.

During the great gale of April, 1851, in which the first Minot's Light was swept down, a number of forty-gallon casks of linseed oil washed ashore at Hull. Because the casks were heavy with barnacles and the iron hoops almost rusted away, it was believed the containers broke away from the disturbed cargo hold of the *Hollander.* The well-aged gin remained at the bottom. Perilous Harding's Ledge is steeped in intoxicating history.

HARRIET ANN - *Only the Clothes on Their Backs*

The *Hingham Journal* recorded a disaster occurring on October 2, 1857:

> *Monday afternoon, about 2 o'clock, schooner* Harriet Ann, *of Lubec [Maine], Captain John Harrington, ran upon the Hardings, and backing off she immediately filled and sunk. Her crew took to the boats and were picked up by the schooner* Bay Queen, *Captain Cobb, for Chatham, and brought to Boston Monday evening. The survivors saved nothing from the schooner but the clothes upon their backs. The* Harriet Ann *was from Philadelphia and was loaded with coal.*

The same news source reported a controversial episode that took place in the Harbor at another time. The master of the ship *Golden Cross,* of Salem, hoisted a distress signal when several sailors rebelled and refused to obey orders. There was even fear that the vessel might be run ashore and wrecked, necessitating strong measures by the captain. The U.S. Revenue Cutter *Morris* rendered assistance, and nine mutineers were placed in irons.

KADOSH - *Wrecked Just Hours after Christmas*

The *Kadosh,* a large bark of 655 tons register, sailing from Yokohama, Japan, and Manila, Philippine Islands, with 500 piculs (a Chinese picul was 133.3

pounds) of sapan wood, 8,920 mats (containers) of sugar, and 2,897 bales of hemp, dragged over Harding's Ledge on December 26, 1872, a few hours after Christmas. Built at East Boston in 1864, the vessel, with a crew of sixteen able-bodied seamen, was under a Captain Matthews on his first voyage as master. With the bark beginning to break up, two boats put off but one swamped, and the captain was lost along with seven men. The navigational instruments, also in the swamped boat, could not be recovered. Two frostbitten stowaways, experiencing their first horrifying sight of ice and snow, were saved.

Tremendous waves continued to batter the *Kadosh* until she went to pieces about in line with the Ledge and Point Allerton. The hemp and wood were salvaged, but the sugar was contaminated. To ward off Pacific Ocean pirates, the bark had one cannon, which was secured from the wreckage. The armament decorated the front lawn of the Village of Hull library for a while. In later years a grateful survivor, in a letter from Australia, remarked that Hull people treated them "as though we were their own sons."

ALICE G. WONSON - *Money Went down with Vessel*

A Boston reporter described a March 6, 1883, wreck:

> *The fishing schooner* Alice G. Wonson *of Gloucester, just returned from a cruise to George's Banks, was caught in the snowstorm while running in for this port on Tuesday, and at 5 P.M. struck on Harding's Ledge with such force as to stave a hole in her bottom. She immediately began to fill and in a few moments disappeared beneath the water, leaving the crew, 14 in number, hardly time to scramble into their dories and pull away from the sinking craft.*
>
> *The Captain states his catch of fish amounted to 70,000 lbs., and but for the unfortunate accident would have made a profit of $350 on this trip. The men saved nothing from the wreck. The Captain had $300 in money in the cabin, and the crew had about $200 on board, all of which went down with the vessel. The schooner was 64 tons register, built in 1870, and was owned by Wm. Perkins Co. of Gloucester.*

H. F. MORSE - *Battered to Bits on Ledge*

"By their brave work of today, Hull's famous and heroic life savers have added new laurels to their already long list of self-sacrificing services." These words appropriately describe a pull of three miles in the surfboat *Nantasket* through seething waters. Captain Samuel James, designer of the

Nantasket and brother of the famed surfman, Joshua, took charge of the rescue effort. The tugboat *H.F. Morse* and a barge were being battered to bits at the Ledge on January 21, 1889. The crew of the tug were successfully removed but told about the sad fate of the barge *Bunyan*.

The barge, which had been only a short distance away, split in half on Harding's. The bargemen were shaken from their handholds, and as three of them floated by the tugboat, pathetic cries for help could be plainly heard. A raging sea meant death for anyone who tried to assist them. The *H. F. Morse* crew, powerless in their own predicament, had to watch them drown.

ENOS B. PHILLIPS - *Fire Built on Deckhouse*

On February 19, 1893, the three-masted schooner *Enos B. Phillips* of Boston, skippered by Captain J. G. Brown, sailing from Baltimore, Maryland, went down between Harding's Ledge and Point Allerton. She had 550 tons of Cumberland coal consigned to the West End Street Railway Company of Boston. Before abandoning the vessel, the captain built a fire of tar and oakum on the deckhouse to alert the lifesaving station. Rowing to shore, they met the Hull surfboat, in which the captain returned to the scene.

The 389-ton schooner's masts, thrusting through the choppy surface, were all they could see, and it was agreed that salvage would be improbable. Captain Brown explained that "it was impossible to estimate his distance from Boston Light because of the blinding snow, that he did not hear the bell buoy, but fearing he was too close to the ledge, he had just changed his course when he struck."

GLENWOOD - *Experience No Match for Gale*

The *Glenwood,* which stranded at Harding's on February 22, 1893, was claimed to be one of the largest and best equipped with navigational aids of perhaps any three-masted schooner afloat. She was 1,649 gross tons, 245 feet long, built in Bath, Maine, owned in Taunton, Massachusetts, and carried 2,444 tons of soft coal for Boston industrial firms. After she struck, soundings found five fathoms aft and three forward. All eleven hands got ashore in the gig and, being fortunate, landed at Allerton Point, where they met a patrol from the lifesaving station.

The captain's twenty years of experience on the high seas had been no match for the wild gale that thrashed his vessel. The *Glenwood* went to pieces, and portions still rest near the site. It is surprising how many ships went to the bottom within view of their Boston waterfront berths.

JOHN ENDICOTT - *Wrecked Steamer Sinks Again*

The attempt to save the excursion steamer John Endicott proved futile, for yesterday [September 16, 1900], while she was being towed up to the city, she again filled off Harding's Ledge, and sank in 10 fathoms of water, where she will probably be allowed to remain. The Endicott was formerly the Stanford, and for many years ran to a number of the harbor resorts, but more especially to Plymouth, from which port she was on her way when she struck one of the ledges off Minot's Light.

With one tug towing and two more alongside pumping, the steamer was gotten under way, and managed to weather Minot's Ledge in spite of the heavy seas. The strain, however, proved too much for her, and when within two miles of the entrance of the harbor, just off famous Harding's Ledge, she suddenly filled and sank.

This account was carried by the *Boston Daily Advertiser.*

J. B. KING & CO. #17 - *Laid Bones on Dangerous Ledge*

The *Boston Globe* of Wednesday, October 21, 1903, told about the wreck of the schooner barge *J. B. King & Co. #17* carrying cement in bags and barrels. "When the tow reached Boston Light Monday evening the number 17, which was the stern barge, was cast off, her instructions being to anchor in the Roads until a harbor tug could tow her to the city. Instead of heading into the Roads, however, she took a sheer and struck on dangerous Harding's Ledge, where so many staunch vessels have laid their bones."

Captain Weter and two seamen packed up their belongings and abandoned the craft, which was obviously a total loss. The ocean tug *Gypsum King* continued on its journey with the three remaining tows. The wrecked barge registered 357 gross tons and was 122.9 feet long. She was constructed in Port Richmond, New York, in 1898.

WYALUSING - *Captain's Error on Clear Night*

About the strange wreck of the sea tug *Wyalusing*, a newsman raised this question: "How the vessel could strike on Harding's on a clear night like Thursday seems inexplicable. The Captain said he was looking out the window on the port side trying to pick up the buoy on Harding's when the tug smashed into the ledge." On April 4, 1906, this workhorse of the sea was shattered near the spot where the tug *H. F. Morse* met its end.

The *Wyalusing* was towing three coal barges, one of which the crew promptly boarded, for a huge hole had been knocked in the tug's hull. Although the vessel's whistle was plainly heard and she could be made out in the darkness, the patrolman at the U.S. Life Saving Service station did not suspect she was in distress. He supposed the craft was anchored for the night to wait for the morning tide. The captain of the tug finally rowed ashore to sheepishly telephone Boston for assistance. The *Wyalusing*, formerly known as the *Governor H. M. White*, was constructed of wood, 118 feet long, and 74 tons.

MOHAVE - *Returning from Submarine Salvage*

The *Boston Post* reported loss of the U.S. Navy tug *Mohave* on February 13, 1928. "Tom was the feline victim of the wreck. His life was snuffed out when the bottom of the *Mohave* was ripped off like so much tissue paper, permitting the heavy seas to flood the radio room where the pet of the crew had been purring on a pile of watch caps and pea jackets. [Wiggles, the canine mascot, was above deck and was rescued by his shipmates.]

"When the ship listed and her hold filled with water, the first consideration was for life, human life. Three men, fearing the ship was about to capsize, launched a small punt and put over the side. It is believed they perished when their small boat swamped."

The 800-ton *Mohave* had been returning from towing pontoons to the salvage site of the U.S. submarine *S-4* off Provincetown, when she plowed into Harding's Ledge. The *S-4* sank to a depth of approximately 110 feet with all hands on December 17, 1927, after a collision with the Coast Guard destroyer *Paulding*. Following extensive salvage operations and widely publicized news coverage, the submarine was finally raised on March 17, 1928.

Point Allerton Shipwrecks

Due west from Harding's Ledge, the long shallow bars of Point Allerton— on occasion identified as Point Alderton—reach out like talons to claw at vessels. Defended by a granite seawall, it is on the northern extremity of Nantasket Beach and opposite the entrance to the Main Ship Channel

M. F. Sweetser states in *Kings Handbook of Boston Harbor*, "Many a good ship has left her bones here to be gnawed away by time and tide." Because shipwrecks were so frequent, a lifeboat and refuge hut were located near the high-water mark.

A number of antiquarians claim that on this headland the Viking chieftain Thorwald received a mortal wound in combat with Indians during the year 1004. Thorwald ordered that he be buried on the point of land, with

Point Allerton, Boston Harbor

a cross at his head and another at his feet, and that it be called Korssanes, which roughly translates to "promontory of the crosses."

From such heights as Point Allerton, during the War of 1812, Hull residents witnessed the battle between the British *Shannon* and American *Chesapeake*, each with thirty-eight guns. The immortal death command by the *Chesapeake*'s Captain Lawrence still echoes over the waters: "Don't give up the ship."

Many skippers were forced to submit to the sea's blows and abandon their vessels on this storm crossroad of Massachusetts Bay.

Twentieth-century gales eventually demolished an ancient beacon on a submerged bar extending in a northerly direction. Ice expanding the seams between granite blocks weakened the pyramidal base. On this unmarked strand the 120-ton colonial vessel *Charity*, with badly needed supplies for an infant Boston, almost came to grief after grounding.

This strategic headland had a military presence during major conflicts from the Revolutionary War to World War II.

Greenough Abbé narrates the salty *History of 79 Point Allerton Avenue*, a former site of the red-shingled Massachusetts Humane Society surfboat house and U.S. Life Saving Service beach patrol checkpoint:

> *The harbor forts [World War I] were manned and engaged in target practice with their nine and twelve inch guns. An Army tug would tow a red triangle target on a raft back and forth across the channel, and the guns would shake the dishes in the pantry and shells would send up geysers of white water. One day something went wrong and a shell landed at the back steps of the house next door. Of course it con-*

> *tained no explosive, but it is nothing you care to have drop into your*
> *living room. The officers from Fort Andrews on Peddocks Island were*
> *embarrassed and very apologetic. They sent a mule team from*
> *Pemberton and invited any of the neighbors to come over to the fort*
> *and see the big guns and how they work.*

With its exposed location and quaint history, the address could well be
called Boston Harbor's "Outermost House."

ELIZABETH - *Harbor Pilot's Heroic Deed*

The brigantine *Elizabeth,* bound from St. Vincents with a Boston consignment, struck the bar off Point Allerton in gale winds on December 15,
1802. Thomas Knox, a harbor pilot, was aboard when she lost her anchor
but was unable to help keep her off. All expected that the *Elizabeth* would
soon go to pieces and they must try to reach shore or perish. Because they
had no boat, Knox, realizing the remaining mariners were debilitated,
decided to swim ashore. He tied an end of a strong line to himself and the
opposite end to the others' bodies. Knox reached the beach in spite of the
billowing sea, and the other survivors were drawn to safety. Hull residents
provided matches and firewood, and the survivors recuperated in a
Massachusetts Humane Society hut-of-refuge. Knox's valor has been emu-
lated by harbor pilots over the decades.

HOOGLY - *The Coffee Ship from Java*

The coffee ship *Hoogly* departed from Batavia, Java, on September 11, 1831,
under Captain Bacon and was hurled ashore in a heavy snowstorm on
Point Allerton's southerly exposure on December 28, 1831. The mizzenmast was cut away to decrease resistance to the wind, preventing her
from heeling over and possibly capsizing. She was loaded with 50,000
piculs of coffee and other assorted cargo. The heavily and richly laden
Hoogly remained tight, and it was assumed she would be got off.
Tradition has it, though, the whitened ribs of the ship lay embedded in
the sand for many years.

EMELINE - *Topsail Schooner Bilged with Loss of Life*

A compassionate Hingham writer in the early 1800s editorialized on the
poor sailor's plight in a typical storm season:

> *It is thought that during the late severe gale . . . a vessel struck upon*
> *some of the rocks in the bay, went to pieces, and all hands were lost, as*

*a man's leg and various fragments of a wreck were washed up on the
beach at Nantasket. Such instances of what is the common fate of mul-
titudes of those who go down to the sea in ships and do business upon
the great waters should awaken the profoundest sympathies of our citizens toward the poor, neglected mariner, and insure good treatment
and fair remuneration for his invaluable services in such a perilous
and hazardous vocation.*

Characteristic of the era, on April 30, 1841, the *Emeline*, a topsail
schooner shipping lumber, bilged in agitated seas on Point Allerton.
Constructed at Charlestown, Massachusetts, she was out of Bucksport,
Maine. A luckless cook and passenger lost their lives in the mishap. The
captain and remaining hands were plucked from the wreckage by the Hull
volunteer lifesavers.

MOHAWK - *Hammered into a Shapeless Wreck*

A typical news account of a wreck revealed:

> *Ship* Mohawk, *of Hallowell, Berry, from Liverpool, October 30, for
> this port dragged ashore on the SE part of Point Allerton about noon
> yesterday. Her masts are gone, and it is probable that she anchored off
> Point Allerton Thursday night during the gale, and she cut her masts
> away when the sea got up to prevent going ashore, but without avail,
> as the sea there has range of the whole bay and breaks very heavily. At
> the last account no one had landed from her and the situation of her
> hull was not known except that she appeared considerably hogged [her
> back was bent]. The* Mohawk *is a good ship of about 350 tons mea-
> surement, built on the Kennebec in 1832, valued at $21,000 and
> insured in this city for $12,000. We did not learn what her cargo is,
> but it is said to be iron.*

The *Mohawk* carried anvils as well as iron, and a case of watches, which
was recovered. The ship was hammered shapeless by the pounding waves.
The Humane Society lifeboat was forced onto the rocks and badly damaged
during this December 17, 1841, rescue, but all the *Mohawk*'s crew survived.

TREMONT - *Another Total Loss*

A brig named *Tremont*, of New York, minus her foresail and foretopsail, was
blown toward shore in the north-northeast gale of October 7, 1844. The
unlucky craft was caught by Point Allerton's bars and held firm to be blud-
geoned by the surf. She was commanded by Captain Leeds, sailing for

Havana, Cuba, with 196 hogsheads, 49 tierces (a tierce was 42 gallons), and 12 barrels of molasses. The wreck was spotted by residents, the Humane Society was alerted, and horses were engaged to transport the lifeboat to the site. One of the deckhands had in the meantime lashed himself to a plank and succeeded in reaching the beach.

After an exhausting row the lifesavers took off the entire crew. In the end the surf broke the brig's deck. The survivors landed at Nantasket, where they were given sustenance. Part of the cargo was expected to be recovered, but she was eventually another total loss.

MASSASOIT - *Indiaman Had Rich Cargo*

The ship *Massasoit,* 395 tons, from Calcutta, India, struck between the Point Allerton bars during a strong northeast tempest on December 11, 1844. Three seamen were drowned in futile attempts to reach land. Great combers broke entirely over the copper-fastened vessel. The Humane Society lifeboat filled with water six times in efforts to approach her. Watching for an opportunity, the surfmen at last succeeded just as *Massasoit* began to break apart. Her stern was soon swept away.

A passenger trying to leave reached the main hatchway, but when the ship lurched suddenly, he fell back into the hatchway. Considering the passenger lost, the lifeboat carrying Captain Barry and other survivors headed for shore. They sighted the passenger crawling on deck, but then the craft broke in half and he toppled into the chasm. Most of the cargo of indigo, silks, shellac, gunny bags, and hides was not recovered. The items were insured for $57,000 with Boston firms.

OLIVER - *Vice-Counsel Learns of Disaster*

Early on the morning of November 20, 1848, the schooner *Oliver* was found near Point Allerton with combers bursting over her. The vessel, captained by William Oliver, out of St. John, New Brunswick, with a load of plaster, lost her entire crew in the misfortune. When the tide ebbed it was learned the *Oliver* had badly bilged, and, as allowed by legal authority, she was sold where she lay, including her cargo.

Salvors assumed that the captain's wife had also succumbed, for a woman's apparel was found in the cabin. The register of the craft washed ashore at the head of Nantasket Beach and was expeditiously delivered to the British vice-counsel in Boston. The documents indicated the *Oliver* was built in 1847 and owned by partners in Albert County, New Brunswick. Trade was so vigorous that wrecks of British vessels were fairly common.

HELENE - *Rated A-1 by Lloyd's of London*

The *Helene,* a schooner headed for Boston from Wilmington, North Carolina, approached the harbor on March 15, 1873. When she was almost parallel to Harding's Ledge, the weather shut down with a thick snowstorm, complicated by a tremendous running sea. The craft passed so close to the northeast bar off Point Allerton that she struck, the tide being low at the time. She continued to strike heavily, the sea making a clean breach over her. The schooner bilged an hour after grounding and drove over the bar.

Captain Adams and his spent crew were taken off in a lifeboat by the Hull volunteers three hours later. Her stern was stove in, the cabin was washed out, and everything belonging to the sailors had disappeared. Fragments of the vessel accumulated along the shore for a mile or more. The cargo of hard pine lumber was salvaged. She was insurance rated A-1 by Lloyd's of London, indicating a vessel in first-class condition.

GRACE LOTHROP - *Savagely Split and Smashed*

The East Boston-owned brig *Grace Lothrop* went aground at Point Allerton on February 1, 1882, shortly after being condemned by board of survey. The vessel, with her cargo of oranges and cigars, was clear of the water when the tide receded, but rough seas had split or smashed the hull in several places, and part of the cargo spilled out. The mariners had been taken off the brig by a towboat and landed at Boston Light.

Another news account indicates the craft was also loaded with 140 tons of logwood from Haiti, West Indies. It is further reported the crew lowered a boat and rowed to shore. The *Grace Lothrop* grated on the rocky beach during the night, being left high and dry at low tide.

After a storm a dropping tide sometimes allowed some cargoes to be salvaged with relative ease, using horse-drawn wagons. The endeavor had to be promptly handled, because the next incoming tide might completely destroy both vessel and merchandise.

BELLE J. NEAL - *Wrecked after Fishing for Months*

The schooner *Belle J. Neal* careened ashore under the granite seawall at Point Allerton on January 3, 1904, ending a Newfoundland fishing expedition begun back in June. The two-master, laden with 22,000 pounds of salt fish, broke up. Captain Osceola F. James of the Massachusetts Humane Society volunteers and Captain William C. Sparrow of the U.S. Life Saving Service picked oarsmen from the two groups to go out to the disaster. Dragging the surfboat *Nantasket* over the rocky shore with extreme hardship, they accomplished the rescue.

The *Belle J. Neal* had almost made it safely into the harbor but lost her sail at the entrance of the south channel. She fell off her course and grounded on the westerly side of the bar. She had also been blown aground on Cape Cod in the November 1888 tempest.

Nantasket Beach Shipwrecks

In a strong onshore gale, the peninsular or upper arm of Nantasket Beach in Hull is as risky as the Point Allerton elbow. (Stony Beach is the forearm on the northern side.) Along Nantasket Beach the surf can be formidable enough to break a wooden ship's keel and smash her to firewood.

The beach also provided the winter's fuel for potbellied stoves from vessels lost near Harding's Ledge. Following a storm an observer said that "teams of every description, cars, wagons, sleds, wheelbarrows, baskets, bags, and buckets were brought into use in gathering the coal that lay scattered all over the sand. Men, women, and children worked with all possible speed to save what they could from the incoming tide. . . . While some of the coal doubtless came from the wrecked schooners, it is claimed that every storm for years has brought in more or less of that which has been lost off the coast."

The bleached framework of several well-known vessels, including the five-masted schooner *Nancy*, have been washed over by innumerable tides. Eventually, the sands swallowed up the remains or they were removed.

Post card depicting the Nancy, *the most famous of Boston Harbor 20th-century wrecks*

How many vessels with ribs splayed like the bones of a split codfish are hidden from view off the shoreline?

Behind long and narrow Nantasket Beach are several elevations: Sagamore Hill, Skull Head, and Strawberry Hill, the latter being most prominent. Parched skeletons allegedly discovered by the first settlers inspired the name Skull Head. A lifeboat was maintained at the base of Strawberry Hill and refuge huts at strategic points. These huts were an oasis in a sandblown desert when stinging gale winds swept Nantasket's shore.

A section of the Hull cemetery had a burial site for unidentified shipwrecked mariners: the "strangers' corner." According to Hull Historical Society President Richard Francis Cleverly, the society will erect a bronze memorial at the site, which will read: "Interred herein are approximately 100 men, women and children known only to God. Victims of shipwrecks on our shores, nearby islands or shoals, from 1860 to 1898."

Craggy Atlantic Hill, where archeologists have unearthed native encampments, is the southern terminus of Nantasket Beach.

Like most other towns, Nantasket had its problems, as we see in this 1856 local newspaper account:

> *Some land pirates, whose souls would rattle in a mustard seed, have been robbing the Humane Houses on Nantasket Beach of the firewood stored therein for the use of the shipwrecked mariners whom the stormy and raging elements would inhospitably throw upon its shore. The crew of the brig which came ashore in the late storm, and who took shelter in one of the Humane Houses on the above beach, were obliged to stand in their wet garments for several hours in consequence to not finding any fuel to light a fire to dry themselves, it having been pilfered by the ruthless vandals who frequent the vicinity, from its lawful and humane receptacle. Such pitiful wretches deserve to be severely dealt with; and we sincerely hope they may be discovered and receive the reward which their baseness merits.*

A windswept blaze broke out at Nantasket pier on Thanksgiving Day in November 1929 and leapt to the steamers *Betty Alden, Mary Chilton, Old Colony, Rose Standish,* and *Nantasket,* all of the Nantasket Beach Line. Only *Mayflower* was saved from the inferno, catastrophic to the town's summer trade.

Facing the open ocean, the Harding's Ledge–Point Allerton–Nantasket Beach complex proved fatal for dozens of vessels. This was the Devil's Triangle of Boston Harbor.

Beautiful Nantasket Beach, Hull, scene of many shipwrecks

ELLSWORTH - *Insurance Expired Before Wreck*

During the February 20, 1837, storm, the brig *Ellsworth* from Rio de Janeiro, with a full hold of coffee, grounded about two miles south of Boston Lighthouse on Nantasket Beach. After she hit, the sea washed away her foremast, main topsail, and all boats. Captain Moses Adams, attempting to get ashore in the anchor chain box, was drowned. Except for the steward, who was also a fatality, the crew landed, but frostbitten.

Although the vessel was insured in Boston for $10,000, the policy had expired a few days before the wreck. Half the bags of coffee were thought to be salvageable, but *Ellsworth* had bilged, and her beams were soundly broken. A vessel in such condition could rarely be refloated.

The face of Nantasket Beach can change from beauty one day to ugly fury on the next, providing a coup de grace to any stranded craft.

LLOYD - *Cargo Strewn on Beach*

On December 23, 1839, the bark *Lloyd* of Portland, Maine, sailing from Havana, approached the harbor in thick weather. Soon after, with masts gone, she struck heavily and was almost swallowed up by the surf on Nantasket Beach. Six of the crew tried to reach safety in a longboat, but it swamped and all perished. Captain Mountford and two others lashed themselves to the mizzen rigging, but waves swept them off. The oldest shipmaster sailing out of Portland and highly respected, Mountford was the last to be pulled under. Of nine men, only one survived: George Scott, a plucky Englishman, was able to swim ashore.

Witnesses were powerless and had to watch waves surge over the bark, dismembering her piece by piece. The cargo was strewn all along the beach, including 80,000 cigars, 536 hogsheads of molasses, and casks of wine. Specie was also said to be in the miscellaneous consignment.

SURPLUS - *Six-Hundred Dozen Eggs*

An unusual and delicate consignment was carried by the schooner *Surplus* of Bristol, Maine, skippered by a Captain Newbert, bound from Waldoboro, Maine, to Boston. In her hold nestled 600 dozen eggs, cords of wood, and bark for the local market. She anchored off Strawberry Hill, Nantasket Beach, under an overcast sky and slowly dragged ashore while the September 25, 1847, storm increased its intensity. The unabated waves cracked her apart, resulting in a complete wreck. The entire crew and passengers were removed by Hull volunteer lifesavers.

Most of the eggs were somehow saved, and the hull, cordwood, and bark were sold at auction right on the beach. When sold in the Boston market, the eggs were said to have been labeled "for scrambled eggs only."

L'ESSAI - *Laden with French Brandy*

The brig *L'Essai*, sailing from Rochelle, France, laden with brandy, anchored off Strawberry Hill in the howling storm of April 8, 1850. Notice was sent from Hull of the vessel's predicament, and the well-known Boston towboat *R.B. Forbes* churned to her aid. Misfortune again struck, for while running out lines, *L'Essai* dragged and went aground on the beach. The masts were cut away to keep her from heeling over, and she fell around toward the wind. A lifeboat was unable to reach her to render assistance.

L'Essai was thrown high up on the sands so that at low tide she was nearly dry. Her sails and rigging were removed, but the vessel could not be hauled off in such strained condition. The master, Captain Duchesne, saved 450 casks of brandy. After makeshift repairs, she was pulled off with great difficulty and towed to Boston.

PEERLESS - *British Schooner Shares the Beach*

The *Hingham Journal and Advertiser* tells the melancholy story of January 4, 1852:

> *During the gale of Sunday, at 1 P.M., the stern post, billet head, spars, timbers, and planks of a vessel came ashore at Nantasket Beach; also the fragments of a boat. The spars and remnants of the boat were painted white; the planks were of beech and birch, and the timbers of hackmatack [tamarack], all of which appeared to belong to a brig of about 200 tons. The crew is supposed to have perished.*
>
> *The British schooner* Peerless, *from New York, of and for St. John, N.B., also went ashore on Nantasket Beach on Sunday, near the Rockland House, but whether she will be got off we have not learned—crew saved. She was in ballast, having only 30 barrels of flour on board. The flour was taken out at low water.*
>
> *On Tuesday last, the pilotboat* Jane *picked up in the harbor, near Lovell's Island, part of a wreck, on which were the words* Alfred Henry *of St. John, N.B. A brig of that name, loaded with coal, is now overdue at Boston.*

HERALD - *Cargo Sweetened Hull Tea*

News of a wreck spread swiftly in small coastal communities such as Hull. A marine tragedy often attracted many people with horsedrawn wagons to assist in any rescue attempts, to observe the frenzied activity, and to glean valuable or useful articles. They gathered thus when the British brig *Herald* was cast up on Nantasket Beach during a blow on January 17, 1859. The cargo included close to 4,000 bags of sugar destined for Boston traders. The sailors were taken off the brig by a lifeboat manned by residents, but the ship, punished unceasingly, proved a total loss.

For many months after the incident, the tea brewed in many Hull homes tasted noticeably sweeter. The *Herald* went aground near the Rockland House, a hotel that stood at the southern end of the beautiful expanse of beach. The Rockland House was known for seafood chowders, fish dinners, and wrecks, which came ashore almost at the doorstep.

W. R. GENN - *Hasty Rescue by Surfmen*

The schooner *W. R. Genn,* deeply laden with coal, was lost on Nantasket

Grand Regatta at Hull

Beach off Strawberry Hill on December 23, 1870. Captain Small reported that he came into Massachusetts Bay at night and ran for Boston. A gale was blowing from north to northeast, accompanied by snow. The first landmark he observed was Nantasket Beach; however, the 145-ton vessel could not come about, and so it struck near the Massachusetts Humane Society hut and remained fast. Seas were boiling over the schooner, and the crew prepared to land in their own boat, but it broke adrift and went ashore empty.

About an hour later the Humane Society lifesavers went to the rescue, but they capsized into the numbing water. On a second heroic attempt they extricated all on board. The rescuers were in such haste that they neglected to inflate the lifeboat floats and had no light, only one bailing bucket, the wrong size steering oar, and no life preservers.

PHANTOM - *House of Refuge Locked*

The crew of the sinking pilot boat *Phantom* scrambled ashore at Nantasket

Beach on the night of January 13, 1874, at the height of a violent snowstorm. The half-frozen men were shocked to find the Humane Society's refuge hut "barred and buttoned." They desperately needed nourishment and protection from freezing, but despite their united efforts they could not get in. After wandering about they discovered telegraph wires, which led them after an exhausting half-mile trek to the Sea Foam House, where treatment was provided. The steward of the *Phantom* was treated for bad frostbite.

Back in January 1857, the *Phantom* had dragged onto the south side of Green Island during a gale. The harbor was frozen almost solid, and the freezing spray gave the ice-coated craft the appearance of a ship of glass.

HARRIET ATWOOD - *Cargo of Oysters Peddled*

At Nantasket Beach the schooner *Harriet Atwood* was wrecked on March 31, 1876. The cargo of fresh oysters was strewn in a heap at midshore, and many Hull residents took the opportunity to lay in a good supply of the bivalves. Several enterprising lads got into temporary business peddling the oysters at 30 cents a bushel through local towns. At the same time, flounders were sold by the bunch, strung on a length of slender tree branch.

Then as today, a tempest deposits on the Nantasket shore such delicacies as lobsters, sea clams, and quahogs. The *Harriet Atwood* was a total wreck but another successful rescue entry on Humane Society records.

BUCEPHALUS - *Deeply Imbedded in Sand*

The *Bucephalus,* a schooner from Provincetown with salted fish, was forced up on the Long Beach section of Hull on February 1, 1882. Her hull was deep in the sand near Ocean House, a favorite summer hotel. Following the storm the vessel stood "as straight and stately as though she was afloat."

The Humane Society archives disclose:

> *On the night of January 31, you will remember that a heavy gale and thick snowstorm prevailed. Boat No. 21 was launched about 2 A.M. Feb. 1st and took off the crew of schooner* Bucephalus *ashore on Nantasket Beach. 8 A.M.—No. 18 took off the crew of schooner* Nettie Walker *ashore about 10 A.M., thus saving many lives and being in the lifeboats some 12 hours in a heavy gale. The Committee recommended that twenty-five dollars be presented to each of the men, viz.: 16 men at $25—amounting to four hundred dollars.*

ANITA OWEN - *A Distress Signal Ignited*

The brigantine *Anita Owen* grounded in the December 1, 1885, northeaster, 300 feet from shore on Nantasket Beach, quickly going to pieces. A distress signal was burned, and had the lifesaving crew not responded quickly, all would have succumbed. Captain Murphy, his wife, and nine seamen were brought ashore.

The vessel had voyaged from Perth Amboy, New Jersey, bound for Portland, Maine, and was caught in the gale outside Boston Harbor. The captain, who had lost his bearings, anchored between Strawberry Hill and Point Allerton, but preventive action was to no avail. The *Anita Owen*, like several other nearby wrecks, had a sizable load of coal. Such heavy cargo weighing down a beached vessel was a great hindrance in refloating it.

ALICE - *Stripped by the Wreckers*

An eye-catching note on activities near Strawberry Hill after the gale on November 25–26, 1888, appeared in a Boston newspaper column. "The brig *Alice* has been completely stripped by the wreckers and others. All that remained this afternoon was the hull, which has been robbed of its copper sheathing and ironwork. The masts were cut away this morning."

The brig, ashore with a general cargo and sugar, was picked clean. The captain later visited the wreck area and warned that "the owners would make efforts to recover all the goods removed, allowing of course lawful salvage to those in whose possession they are found." The value of the *Alice* was $5,000, covered by adequate insurance. Miscellaneous cargo consigned to the Provinces had a value of $8,000 to $10,000. Reclaiming material from Hull homes would itself cause a tempest.

H. C. HIGGINSON - *Ashore near Lobster Rock*

Another wreck in the infamous November 1888 storm was that of the schooner *H. C. Higginson,* transporting plaster. She came in on Nantasket Beach near Lobster Rock, which is at the base of Atlantic Hill. Attempts to rescue the crew by breeches buoy failed. The surfboat *Nantasket* came to the mariners' aid and, after a hard pull against the currents, reached the schooner. Sailors in the rigging, spent from long exposure, were barely able to catch ropes thrown to them, slide down the breeches-buoy line from foremast to mizzenmast, and then jump into the breakers to be hauled into the surfboat. Three of the men on the three-master lost their lives. The captain and one other man had been washed overboard before the Humane Society volunteers arrived. A third individual, lashed to the rigging, died there from exposure. His wife stood on a ledge overlooking the scene and pitifully called to him to sustain his feeble hold on life.

In the bleakest winter rescues the lifesavers had to literally chop from the rigging mariners who were frozen in statuelike poses.

Schooner H.C. Higginson **(Courtesy: Richard M. Boonisar)**

MATTIE E. EATON - *Lashed to the Rigging*

The Reverend Dr. A. N. Plumb told of his son's experience on the three-masted schooner *Mattie E. Eaton* of Thomaston, Maine. Headed for Trinidad, she was wrecked opposite the Pavilion at Nantasket Beach. "My son was going away for the winter. They got off well, but carried away a top-mast and had to put back for repairs. From 10 o'clock till 2 they were lashed to the rigging, the sea breaking over them. At 2 o'clock she beached, narrowly grazing the rocks. The rocks carried away her rudder. Providentially, the schooner drifted upon the sand. At daybreak a line was got ashore. The ship's boat had been lost, but the captain's dory was used, and with the aid of many friends ashore all were brought away from the wreck safely."

The new vessel, with a consignment of ice and general goods, was wrecked 1,500 feet northwest of the *H. C. Higginson* in the same November storm.

Remains of the Schooner Cox & Green, *Hull, Mass.* (**Courtesy: Society for the Preservation of New England Antiquities**)

MARY A. HOOD - *Scattered Cargo on Strawberry Ledge*

The schooner *Mary A. Hood* was wrecked in fourteen feet of water on April 9, 1894, as described in a U.S. Life Saving Service report:

> *Anchored off Nantasket Beach in easterly gale and snowstorm 3 P.M., but soon began dragging ashore. Launched Massachusetts Humane Society's surfboat, which was close at hand, having two volunteers besides station crew, but found it impossible to reach her. Again launched with station crew and five volunteers at the oars and reached her just as she stranded. Rescued her crew of six persons and took them to station where they remained till the afternoon of the 10th instant. Vessel broke up soon after stranding, becoming a total loss.*

Loaded with iron water pipe, the *Mary A. Hood* scattered her cargo near Strawberry Ledge, a few hundred yards off the shoreline.

ULRICA - *Lifesaving at Age Seventy*

A three-masted schooner of 298 tons, bound for Hoboken, New Jersey, with plaster, the *Ulrica,* came ashore and became a wreck near the Surfside House, Kenberma vicinity of Nantasket, on December 16, 1896. Part of the U.S. Life Saving crew arrived on the scene by flagging down the local train. Captain Joshua James, the station keeper, was washed out of the surfboat *Nantasket* in a rescue effort, but grabbed an oar as the boat passed over him. A news clipping of the event reads: "Few men of his age, however, for he is 70, could pass through the exposure and excitement he has today without serious results. The wonderful man is tonight as physically able to pass, at a moment's notice, through another ordeal with any man of his crew, and with pride every one of them admit it. It was even with reluctance that he was induced to take stimulants, for during his long life the Captain has abstained from the use of liquor and tobacco."

The lifesaving gun proved unsuccessful, for the half-frozen sailors clinging to the vessel were too exhausted to fasten the line high enough to keep it out of the foaming waves. On the fourth surfboat attempt, the line was used to help guide the *Nantasket* to the wreck.

NANCY - *Famed Five-masted Schooner*

> *Nantasket—Feb. 20 (1927)—At the height of the severe northeast gale at 1:40 this afternoon with the wind blowing 70-odd miles an hour and big breakers rising to the height of eight to 15 feet, the five-masted schooner* Nancy *of Philadelphia, which had anchored outside the Boston Lightship, was driven ashore with anchors dragging at Long Beach, between White Head and Surfside. The entire crew, nine men, was rescued by Captain O. F. James and picked crew the famous life-saver enlisted from the crowd of residents who rushed to the beach when the* Nancy *grounded.*

Further research in local news articles discloses that the vessel, launched at Portland, Oregon, in 1918, served the French Army, and was to become known as the most controversial wreck at Hull. Having just discharged her cargo of coal at Boston, she had an empty hold and was bound for Norfolk. It was claimed that all three anchor chains and cable had snapped one by one in the heavy seas. A hastily raised foresail gave the *Nancy* sufficient steerage under the hand of her skipper, E. M. Baird, to narrowly avoid striking on treacherous Thieves Ledge. She had barely cleared the ledge when the sail blew apart. A minute sooner and the entire crew might have gone down with the vessel. Speculation spread on details about causes behind the big schooner's going ashore.

The stately vessel remained intact and upright well above the tides for

The Nancy *was indeed a beautiful specimen.* (**Courtesy: Peabody Museum of Salem**)

several years, a great attraction for sightseers and subject for armchair navigators. Visitors were allowed on board the five-sticker for 25 cents. Even after the *Nancy* caught fire, and was eventually demolished, the charred remains were a Nantasket landmark.

Stony Beach and Toddy Rocks Shipwrecks

From Point Allerton the Main Ship Channel's (Nantasket Roads) southern shores extend westward to Hull Gut. A rather narrow half-mile rocky strip, Stony Beach, connects the Point with higher elevations in Hull, the Nantasket Hills. These heights, including the present Telegraph Hill, have clifflike eroded faces on their northern sides and are protected by a granite seawall. Many whistle-calls of distress have reverberated off these hillsides. At low water, particularly on Quarter Ledge, large boulders are

HUMANE SOCIETY OF MASSACHUSETTS.

USE OF BOAT.

WRECK REPORT.

STATION No. *21*

NAME OF VESSEL,

Nancy

DATE OF DISASTER,

Feb. 20. 1927

DATE OF REPORT, *Feb 21. 1927*

Osceola F. James KEEPER.

Humane Society wreck report (Courtesy: Richard M. Boonisar)

revealed well off the beach. A map engraved for the *American Coast Pilot*, published by E. and G. W. Blunt in 1841, labeled this area Warter Ledge. Toddy Rocks, close to the edge of the main channel, were the primary culprit in splintering several staunch hulls. A well-equipped lifesaving station with its identifiable red roof was just over the crest of Stony Beach, an advantageous position from which to watch the main channel and surrounding islands, and to launch a rescue attempt. The station now holds the Hull Lifesaving Museum.

Following the British evacuation of Boston, the summit of Telegraph Hill, heavily fortified by American militia and French marines, had hot exchanges of fire with British frigates. With armaments thrusting out of powder-blackened embrasures on these domineering heights, it was a classic citadel from our Revolutionary War period.

After the Revolution a signal station inside the fort was responsible for sending semaphore, and, later, magnetic telegraph messages to the Boston Merchants Exchange, advising of approaching ships of commerce and alerting officials about marine disasters. What tragic tales of storm havoc the telegraph key must have tapped out.

A typically brief account of such a message appeared in the *Boston Post:* "The outer telegraph station yesterday afternoon reported that the brig *Charles Wells,* which sailed from Philadelphia for this port, 24th-ULT., probably coal laden, and owned by John Wade and others, went to pieces (November 5, 1839) on Long Beach, Nantasket, and all hands perished."

From 1824 to 1840 the signal station reported 28,155 incoming vessels to the observatory at Central Wharf, Boston, but this figure did not include smaller coasting craft. Before the telegraph was installed, sets of

The U.S. Life Saving Service Station, Hull, was constructed in 1889.
(Courtesy: Hull Lifesaving Museum)

flags for each of 112 Boston shipping merchants were displayed to identify incoming craft. It was certainly a unique and colorful arrangement. The hilltop perch must have been quite similar to the crow's nest of a tall-masted vessel, allowing for a bird's-eye view of Massachusetts Bay.

The *Hingham Journal* reported that during the tempest of January 13, 1856: "The wind was from the northeast, and so high on the seashore that no man could stand before it. As the marine telegraph was broken in several pieces, and it was found impossible to repair it, the individuals who have charge of the telegraph station at Hull started for Boston in a sleigh, to give intelligence of the state of things on the shore." Meanwhile, several wrecks occurred on the harbor islands.

Old Fort Independence on Telegraph Hill was later renamed Fort Revere, which was an active military installation during World Wars I and II. Its arsenal initially ranged from immense barbette guns, mounted on a platform or mound high enough to fire over parapets, to armor-piercing rapid-fire cannon on disappearing carriages. Eventually antiaircraft guns with supporting searchlights were added.

The Nantasket Beach Railroad, which ran along the Hull coastline and the base of the hill, was sometimes employed by the U. S. Life Saving Service for transporting lifeboats and other equipment to disaster sites. In the February 1882 blow, the schooner *Nettie Walker* thrashed onto Stony

Magnetic Telegraph Station, Telegraph Hill, Hull

Beach, ripping up sections of track while coal gushed from a hole in her side. Proof of the sea's power was displayed at one point where a mammoth boulder, estimated to weigh five tons, was deposited on the rails.

A steeple or two penetrating the skyline distinguished the antiquated hamlet of Hull, tucked away just south of Telegraph Hill. These landmarks often served skippers as navigational reference points.

In an 1848 pamphlet, *Notes on the Sea Shore*, James Lloyd Homer reminisces:

> *Some of the Hullonians are in the habit of buying wrecks and then breaking them up, saving the iron, copper, and such other parts as are valuable, and using the wood for fuel. The wreck of the ill-fated* Massasoit *and that of the brig* Tremont, *cast away last winter at Point Alderton, have been entirely broken up and the materials are piled up mountain high before the house of Mr. Mitchell, who has enough of*

this kind of stuff to load a ship of three hundred tons. He is a wholesale dealer in wrecked vessels, in old masts, spars, rigging, iron, and brass.

The wreck of the old brig Favorite *lies upon the beach, as does that of the schooner* Emeline. *Both vessels, heavily laden, were sunk some three or four years since, off Nantasket Beach, and afterwards raised by Mitchell and others, on shares, and towed into Hull Bay. The hull of the* Favorite *at low water was formerly used as a shelter for horses when the stable of Mr. Tower was full; it is now too deeply imbedded in the sand for that purpose.*

There are numerous relics of the old ship Mohawk, *which was wrecked off P. Alderton with a valuable cargo from Liverpool; her figurehead decorates one of Mr. Mitchell's buildings; her roundhouse he uses as a counting room and for other purposes.*

The town is exceedingly rich in maritime lore. Numerous vessels have been dashed to pieces on the shoreline's jagged rocks or grinding sands. Figureheads and quarterboards graced a number of buildings, adding a picturesque dash. Several artifacts identifying wrecked craft were nailed to the bandstand near the center of Hull.

James H. Stark commented in his *Illustrated History of Boston Harbor* (1879): "In many places along the beach, timbers of wrecked vessels are

Hull Gut from Peddock's Island

met with, deeply imbedded in the sand, the ribs of which, in projecting out of the sand, have the appearance of formidable teeth belonging to some sea monster."

The frequent calamities, some of the severest occurring at or near Stony Beach and Toddy Rocks, greatly lengthened the harbor's list of wrecks.

HEPZIBAH - *Sank like a Stone*

A sorrowful accident struck the sloop *Hepzibah* on April 3, 1837. Returning from Boston through Hull Gut, the vessel was engulfed by a sudden squall and thrown on her beam ends by a flaw of wind. She sank like a stone before Mrs. William James and other family members trapped in the cabin could be pulled free. The brave woman had gone below to save one of her children and grandchildren. The sloop belonged to a son whom she had rescued from a well when he was a child. Mrs. James was the mother of Joshua James, then only ten and destined to become America's most illustrious lifesaver. Joshua cherished his mother and mourned her passing. One of his sisters commented, "Ever after that he seemed to be scanning the sea in quest of imperiled lives."

With currents reaching several knots, Hull Gut is considered an extremely hazardous passage.

DELAWARE - *Tide Ebbed and Flowed through Ship*

The 600-ton ship *Delaware* of Bath, Maine, valued at $25,000 and carrying cotton, grounded two cable lengths from shore at Stony Beach on March 2, 1857. She bilged so badly that the tide ebbed and flowed right through her. A surfboat safely took off Captain Pattern and all hands. The skipper reported that on Sunday, just after midnight, the *Delaware* was thirty-five miles east of Boston Light. At 8:00 P.M., with the lighthouse about ten miles away, she shortened sail and hove to.

About 11:00 P.M., as the northeast wind increased, the fore and main topsails were close reefed and the mizzen topsails taken in. At 1:00 A.M. Monday, because the vessel was drifting westward, it became necessary to run for the harbor or go ashore. At 4:00 A.M., she anchored in Nantasket Roads. The masts had to be cut away at 9:30 A.M., and an hour later the *Delaware* beached, but the crew was rescued.

The brig *Lorana,* loaded with sugar, went ashore nearby in the same storm, but was refloated.

ODESSA - *Hit Sandspit in a Snowstorm*

Also on March 2, 1857, the British brig *Odessa* hit the sandspit extending off Boston Light during a heavy snowstorm. The crewmen immediately took refuge at the lighthouse, anticipating that the brig would break up on the shoal. Unexpectedly, increased wind velocity forced the brig over the spit, across several hundred yards of open water, and high onto Stony Beach, Hull, knocking off the keel. When the storm abated, the crew, commanded by a Captain Hilton, landed from the lighthouse to initiate salvage on Stony Beach.

The *Odessa* had sailed from Fortuna Bay, Newfoundland, with a cargo of herring. To this day, timbers from wreckage can be found here, grim reminders of past maritime calamities.

SWORDFISH - *Brig Bound for Cuba*

The Matanzas, Cuba-bound brig *Swordfish* was wrecked on Toddy Rocks on February 17, 1884, with a cargo of lumber. She was at anchor in Nantasket Roads, parted her anchor chains in high winds, and was forced ashore. The British craft bilged and lost her rudder; the waves were so formidable that she could not be boarded. A report issued three days later indicated that although full of water, she was hauled off the rocks by a party of wreckers from Hull. The steamer *Huron* towed her up to East Boston for repairs.

A vessel listed in newspapers or other documentation as a total or complete wreck was occasionally salvaged almost intact. Successful recovery efforts often failed to appear in print, or descriptions were fragmented. The news media, though, are normally the best source of information on early disasters.

COX & GREEN - *Catastrophic Storm of 1888*

The *Cox & Green* of Greenport, New York, was wrecked 200 feet from shore on the west side of Toddy Rocks, on the 25th, during the great storm of November 25–26, 1888. Captain Henry Thompson described the disaster: "We sailed from Philadelphia, Wednesday last, bound for Boston, with a load of coal for Mystic Wharf, Chelsea. We had good weather. We anchored in Nantasket Roads at about 11:30 Saturday night. Sunday morning we began to drift and struck on the rocks about noon. The mainmast went overboard in the night, and Sunday afternoon the foresail and forestay-sail were blown away."

The crew was taken off by means of the Hunt gun and breeches buoy,

Schooner Cox & Green *dismembered by gale* (**Courtesy: Mariners Museum, Newport News, VA**)

high above the waves, as the ocean began to tear the craft apart. The schooner, carrying 700 tons of coal, was constructed at Newburyport, Massachusetts, in 1881. In addition to coal, wrecks such as this frequently replenished the villagers' supply of firewood as well as coal, keeping out the New England winter chill.

GERTRUDE ABBOTT - *U.S. Congress Bestows Gold Medals*

On November 25, 1888, the schooner *Gertrude Abbott*, out of Philadelphia, laden with 823 tons of coal, grounded on the eastern edge of Toddy Rocks. She was about one-eighth mile from the schooner *Cox & Green*. A distress signal was immediately hoisted. The Massachusetts Humane Society surfboat *R. B. Forbes,* commanded by Captain Joshua James, reached the wreck site against heavy odds. The surfboat was so crowded upon returning that the crew had little space for working the oars.

Two hundred yards from shore the lifeboat struck a boulder, almost capsizing in the seething surf. One man fell overboard but was hauled back before being swept away. Huge rocks were grazed and oars were shattered, but with the grace of God they landed safely, though one side was stove in.

At this notorious wreck site, Captain James warned volunteers that chances were they would never return from the rescue attempt; every man offered himself without hesitation. By act of the U.S. Congress, gold medals were bestowed upon the lifesavers.

Boston Lightship, 1915. Photograph by N.L. Stebbins **(Courtesy: Society for the Preservation of New England Antiquities)**

BERTHA F. WALKER - *Captain and Mate Washed Overboard*

A survivor told about a schooner's tragic loss.

> *The* Bertha F. Walker, *in from Philadelphia with a cargo of 975 tons of coal, Captain Westgate of Berkley, Massachusetts in command. We came into the roads about midnight Saturday. We lay securely till about 10 o'clock, when the anchor began to drag, and we drifted all day till about 10 o'clock Sunday night when we struck on the rocks. We all crawled under the forecastle deck where we stayed until early Monday morning when the waves breaking over the vessel forced us to take to the rigging.*
>
> *Captain Westgate and mate Thomas of Isleboro, Maine, waited till all the men were safe aloft before they tried to get a place of safety. But they had waited too long and were washed overboard. We remained aloft till taken off by the life saving crew. The vessel was a total wreck.*

This schooner calamity also occurred at Toddy Rocks during the November 1888 storm, on the 25th, and a few hundred yards northwest of the *Gertrude Abbott* wreck.

ABEL E. BABCOCK - *Only Wreck's Ribs Visible*

Commanded by Captain Babcock, the *Abel E. Babcock* of Philadelphia beat heavily on rough bottom just off Stony Beach. An observer wrote: "Nothing but the ribs of the frame can be seen above the waves and nothing has been seen of the five men who constituted the crew." The Pennsylvania coaler, a small four-master, had come ashore in towering combers during November 27, 1898, one of the worst days in Boston Harbor history. Most of her cargo of coal was recovered. While off the tip of Cape Cod, the captain had turned down a tow to Boston. This aid could have been his salvation.

Apparently the skipper had been able to make Boston Lighthouse in the teeth of the gale and continued his approach to make the lee side of an inner island. The raging wind and strong currents, however, could not be overcome. The storm caused terrible damage to roads, piers, cottages, and the small railroad depot at Stony Beach.

Following the tempest, the Boston Harbor Police surveyed the destruction, observing: "The bones of many vessels bleached on the shore."

HENRY R. TILTON - *Sea Submerged Surfmen*

At the height of the November 1898 storm, on the 27th, the schooner *Henry R. Tilton* was dashed ashore just west of Toddy Rocks. An official U.S. Life Saving Service report reveals: "Parted chains during the hurricane and stranded near the station. Surfmen, assisted by the Massachusetts Humane Society volunteers, took the beach apparatus abreast of her and soon had a

line aboard her. The gear being set up, surfmen landed all seven of the crew without accident. The sea was very heavy and at times washed over the seawall, submerging the surfmen and their apparatus. Succored the shipwrecked men at the station for four days. The vessel was lost."

Another account indicated that the three-masted vessel was eventually pulled off by tugs. The schooner's sizable load of lumber helped keep her afloat and allowed the combers to push the craft well within range of the breeches-buoy equipment.

Schooner Henry R. Tilton *on Stony Beach, Hull, after the Great Storm of November, 1898*

Outer-Islands Shipwrecks

The confined Main Ship Channel, also known as Lighthouse Channel or Nantasket Roads, runs between Point Allerton and Little Brewster Island, on which historic Boston Light penetrates the skyline. Shipwrecks off Boston in the 1600s and early 1700s prompted a Lighthouse Construction Act, which was passed in 1715. The legislation emphasized that "the want of a Lighthouse at the entrance to the Harbor of Boston has been a great discouragement to navigation by the loss of the lives and estates of several of His Majesty's subjects."

The lighthouse, first in the nation, went into operation on September 14, 1716, and in time was furnished with an iron cannon to answer fog-bound ships. A bell was also at hand to be rung in thick weather. Foghorns had difficulty penetrating the occasional wall of mist a few miles east of Boston Light, which was aptly called the Ghost Walk. The lighthouse served as a duty house for pilots because it was the most advantageous place for spotting incoming craft. A tax was levied against shipping to off-set the beacon's expense.

Set ablaze by both combatants during the Revolutionary War, the light-house required major renovations. Patriot Samuel Bixby recorded in his 1775 diary: "August 1st. Yesterday we had a fight with the regulars down at the lighthouse. We killed a considerable number of them, made prisoners of 35 regulars and 7 Tories, burnt two schooners, one house and one barn, sank one barge and took a great deal of plunder." The light was again

The Outer Harbor, from Fort Warren

extinguished during World War II, but only to ensure that the glow would not guide enemy ships or aircraft.

Over the centuries many courageous keepers—and their equally brave wives—have devotedly tended the famed lantern. Their rescue efforts would indeed fill a volume. Furthermore, they sometimes had helpers: About the turn of the century, Nellie, an intelligent and powerful St. Bernard, warned the lighthouse occupants of any vessel in danger off the shore of the island by her continuous barking.

A 1916 *Boston Evening Transcript* article notes: "Boston Light, for many years, was the landing place of the famous boarding house runners. These picturesque denizens of the city used to congregate on the Brewster, each day, awaiting the approach of ships, when they would dash out in their longboats in the Roads to lure sailors to their dens and there attempt to separate them from the fruits of their toil. They were a hardened lot, most of them, piratical-looking blackguards 'whose very language,' asserts one contemporaneous authority, 'would have secured them a hanging at the hands of the original settlers along the harbor.'"

The present lantern is 102 feet above sea level, with almost 2,000,000 candlepower, with 336 glass prisms in a five-ton Fresnel lens, and can be seen from a distance of twenty-seven miles. With the panoramic vista, the lighthouse crew, among other duties, provides weather reports, monitors navigational aids, and checks on the safety of craft in the vicinity.

An old issue of the *Marine Journal* described the contemporary structure: "It is of rough boulder stone, hooped with iron bands, and its clean whitewashed form is a landmark and seamark far and wide. A rusty iron railway for carrying coal leads up from the water side to the engine house, where there is an engine and boilers in which steam is kept up continually to operate the siren fog horns. Their great trumpetlike forms protrude through the wall of the building on the seaward side. In foggy weather one can hear from the open window the far-off mooing of the fog horn on the Boston lightship seven miles away, as the keepers on the lightship can hear this one at Boston Light."

Treacherous Shag Rocks, formerly known as Egg Rocks or Bald Rocks, lie about a half-mile east of Little Brewster Island. The group of bare rocks, etched by sea and wind, extends a third of a mile and juts about twenty-five feet above the high-tide mark.

One of the most tragic harbor wrecks occurred here when the ship *Maritana* and twenty-six persons were lost in 1861. The *Maritana*'s figurehead was originally mounted on a French vessel captured in 1798, then installed on *Caroline*, an American ship that met disaster in New England waters. The jinxed figurehead was recovered, only to be involved in the *Maritana* calamity.

In many a major storm, a dim hull outline might be seen on Shag Rocks, the deck wreathed in foam, tattered sails and flailing ropes snapping like whips, while the vessel's bell tolled its own dirge.

Half a mile north of Shag Rocks, Great Brewster Island rises abruptly, presenting a waterworn face on the ocean flank. This island, with nearby Middle Brewster, Outer Brewster, Calf, Little Calf, and Green, form a natural outer breakwater to help protect the inner harbor against the sea's buffeting. The rugged isles are often engulfed, though, by the elements. They resemble the rough Maine coast, and it is a delight to roam their weather-beaten shores.

Mid-1800s *Atlantic Coast Pilot Directions* described Great Brewster:

> *On passing Harding's Ledge beacon, Boston Lighthouse will be seen directly ahead and on with the southern end of a remarkable looking island, which looks like Point Allerton, except that the high, horned hill is at its northern end, and the sharp peak like the pommel of a saddle at its southern end. But the perpendicular cliffs and the grassy surface are exactly similar to those on Point Allerton. This is Great Brewster. So exactly similar has the action of the sea been on this island and Point Allerton that they appear as if they had formerly been joined together and afterwards separated by some great convulsion of nature.*

Portions of Great Brewster Island are reinforced with a seawall to halt erosion by the waves. The island supplied stone and gravel ballast for hundreds of sailing craft.

Elaborate plans were drawn up for torpedo-launching chutes when America was embroiled in the Spanish-American War. During World War II, a command post for an electronically operated harbor minefield was part of the defenses. Also, rapid-fire 90-millimeter guns were emplaced to fend off any torpedo boats the enemy might attempt to deploy.

False Spit Bar, which is dry at low tide, juts from the southwest side of Great Brewster and extends westward for three-quarters of a mile to The Narrows. Bug Light was a hexagonal structure on iron stilts with a fixed red warning beacon visible for seven miles, illuminated on August 1, 1856. Looking like a huge water insect, it was at the end of the spit. The light, thirty-five feet above the sea, was designed as a guide for clearing the spit, and when in range with Long Island Head Light, would take a vessel clear of Harding's Ledge. It was totally destroyed by fire in 1929. During a heavy gale, it was said, stones would hammer against the structure's legs and the occupants could hear unusual musical scales, much like being inside a huge iron xylophone.

Northeasterly of Great Brewster are the rocks of Middle Brewster, with

Bug Light and Fort Warren, Boston Harbor

several cliffs plummeting into the sea. The winds struck this exposed island with such force as to require propping up fishermen's cottages with supporting timbers. Often the residents built their dwellings with bits and pieces of wreck materials. A modern U.S. Coast and Geodetic Survey chart shows symbols indicating a number of wrecks in the vicinity. Most of these were barges that could no longer take the abuse heaped upon them.

A narrow and dangerous passage, the Flying Place, separates Middle Brewster from Outer Brewster. A few sailors knew it as Outward Island. The site is enchanting, with coves, fissures, and chasms. An early landmark for navigators was known as easternmost tree, which was near North Point. Lonely trees were primary navigational aids when wending a course through the islands. Some have said that the spirit of the wind resides at this mystical island. An extraordinary rock formation near the western-most cove was named the pulpit, from which a nineteenth-century histori-an claims "the Rev. East Wind delivers very powerful addresses."

During World War II, the army could voice its own sermons with a for-tified battery of radar-controlled six-inch artillery. Outer Brewster, with bomb- and chemical-proof concrete bunkers, was known in military circles as the Corregidor of New England.

A prior owner cut an artificial channel into the eastern end of the island as a haven for small boats. A heavy wooden gate once shut out rough waters from the minuscule harbor.

Barren Calf Island, west of Outer Brewster and due north from Great

Brewster, according to the *King's Handbook of Boston Harbor,* is "punctured with caves and fissures which give weird tongue to the wind and waters." On the island was the summer residence of actress Julia Arthur, called the Sarah Bernhardt of America. A visiting columnist reported: "Sometimes when the dismal wail of the fog horn penetrates the smother of the angry night, it seems to the imaginative guests who come to enjoy the hospitality of Mr. and Mrs. Julia Arthur Cheney as if all the dead men ever made dead by the Shags, the Graves, the Roaring Bulls, the dread Harding's Ledge, and other sea dangers at the harbor's rim had combined in one last, dreadful cry of despair."

Calf was the scene of shipwreck and allegedly is the burial place for several seamen. At one time a Massachusetts Humane Society refuge hut was at the southwest end of the island. In older days, it appeared on some charts as Apthorp's Island.

Only a few dozen yards north of Calf, the scarred ledges of Little Calf Island break the mighty rushes of white combers. As on Calf, the graves of a few sailors cast up by the sea many, many years ago are said to be on this island.

The northernmost of the outer rocky sentinels is Green Island, in earlier times named North Brewster. The solitary pilothouse of a wrecked coal barge has long since disappeared, perhaps burned by stranded mariners. Hypocrite Channel flows in swift tidal currents between Green and Little Calf. A range of sawtoothed, uptilted ledges fences the southeast side of Green Island. These island dots have been haunted by nebulous legends. They were sometimes occupied by a hermit or lobsterman, who might haul a castaway from dashing seas. The present squatters are nesting gulls and other aquatic birds.

Some fascinating stretches of sea bottom lie near the outer islands, giving the locale distinct potential for an underwater park. The sea in this area has fairly good visibility; there are a variety of marine fauna, numerous fish and crustacean species, and the remains of shipwrecks.

The kelp-covered Graves Ledge supports the easternmost lighthouse in Boston Harbor. Graves Light was built in 1903, primarily to help watch over the newly dredged Broad Sound Channel. It is ninety-eight feet above sea level and its range is twenty-four miles.

A journalist exploring the Graves provided details:

Seven stories of lighthouse intervene between the first opening, forty feet up, and the top of the lantern, a storeroom, full of emergency supplies of coal and wood against a possible demolition of the magazine; an engineroom for the operation of the foghorn; a kitchen as compact as a steamer's galley, and rather more neat; two bedrooms, one above anoth-

er; the floor of the parapet, and balcony, and the lantern. White tiled brick, a mahogany stair rail, bronze and quartered oak, and profusion of brass work combine their touches of ornament and elegance about the place to deprive it of the official coldness which often causes public institutions to suggest the chill barrenness of a prison. The rooms in the Graves are reminiscent of cheery, compact little cabins on a smart steamer.

With all the breastworks of ledges and islands, even a military strategist could not have planned a harbor with such a fearful array of natural defenses.

Just southwest of Graves Light, the Roaring Bull's reef curves toward Green Island. A few vessels have been on the horns of dilemma at this reef. The Graves Light ramparts get the full brunt of northeast gales. The ledge, visible mostly at low tide, is several hundred yards long.

A smaller ledge, the Northeast Graves, is hidden about 450 yards from the lighthouse. The Northeast Graves was previously marked with a large whistling buoy sounded by the motion of the waves. The pilot boat *Hornet* was run down and sunk off this ledge in June 1854 by the brig *Clement*, but no lives were lost.

Most historians say the Graves is not named as the last resting place for shipwrecked sailors but for Admiral Thomas Graves, who commanded colonial-era vessels. We can only guess how many ships and human lives disappeared without trace over the centuries.

The old Dumping Grounds buoy was anchored in eighteen fathoms, about three and five-eights miles and thirty-five degrees from Graves Lighthouse. Many vessels no longer serviceable were towed to this area just beyond the outer harbor and scuttled. Among these were the packet *King Philip*, trawlers *Ocean* and *Wave*, freighters *Massasoit* and *Coyote*, schooner *Ethel*, sloop *Mary A. White*, and *Eagle Boat #42*. Usually, the discards were stripped of everything valuable before the final plunge. They went down within sight of the *Boston Lightship*, a lonely sentinel off the outer harbor. The first of several guardians went on duty in 1894.

An official government reference work lists the *Sarah Wood* as wrecked at Boston Light on October 10, 1911. As such stories sometimes turn, however, an obituary in the *Boston Evening Transcript* told a different story: "Old Schooner is Buried—'Davy Jones' has at last claimed the old schooner *Sarah Wood*. The little two-master which for nearly sixty years survived the elements, was buried in the Bay today. She was towed from East Boston yesterday, but upon reaching Shirly Gut a strong tide made it necessary to anchor. Upon reaching the spot chosen for her grave today the chains

The Graves Light, Boston Harbor

holding her to pontoons were slipped from under her hull and she sank in twenty fathoms."

The old wooden steamer *Coyote,* a 267-foot eyesore on the Apple Island flats, was pulled off by tugs on January 11, 1932, and went to her last port in deep water off the lightship. To ensure that she would stay on the bottom, two boilers, the crankshaft, and the propeller were not removed. Fifty pounds of dynamite set off in her innards for good measure sent the vessel down.

According to the Boston Port Authority, the *Coyote* was to be the first of sixty-four hulks removed from the harbor.

The *Boston Lightship,* which was formerly stationed about five miles seaward of the Graves, was struck by the British freighter *Seven Seas Spray* on December 20, 1935, when the latter's steering mechanism failed. The freighter, carrying scrap iron, cut a huge wound midship on the lightship's port side "which was staunched with bags of coal." Because the bags kept the sea from flooding the craft, she made port for repairs and was soon back on duty.

Boston Lightship was bravely manned by U.S. Coast Guardsmen during World War II, although it was a sitting duck for U-boats.

Harbor enthusiast and yachtsman James Dean, once president of the Boston Stock Exchange, realizing how monotonous life aboard the vessel could be, stipulated in his will that a $10,000 fund be set up for delivering Boston Sunday newspapers. Mr. Dean, who died in 1942, personally delivered the newspapers, weather permitting, every Sunday for his last fifteen years.

UNIDENTIFIED BRIG - *Cargo Spiced with Treasure*

A calamity that interests treasure hunters is an unidentified brig dashed to smithereens at Shag Rocks on December 4, 1768. The brig, sailing from the West Indies, was captained by Thomas Morton, hailed from Boston, and carried sugar and molasses; the cargo allegedly was spiced with a chest of gold and silver coin. The sailors were safely brought ashore, though with difficulty; however, we have no known record that the chest was recovered by wreckers or later divers.

Salvage would have been difficult, especially with the rapid tidal sweep. Also, wreckage would probably have been carried away in the surge of water. Limited surveys of the surrounding ocean floor have failed to uncover treasure.

OLIVE BRANCH - *Disaster on Devil's Back*

Disaster overtook the schooner *Olive Branch* on Devil's Back on May 11, 1827. The vessel, carrying wood, hay, leather, and butter was thrust in bad weather into Broad Sound under bare poles, having split the foresail and topsail. As she beat over the ledge, both anchors were released and inadequate pumps put into action. Except for a passenger who sought safety on the quarterdeck and was swept off, Captain Samuel Adams, three seamen, and four passengers took to the rigging. One passenger soon lost his hold and was seen no more.

The pilot boat *Favorite* under Captain Reuben Coombs battled high winds and seas in responding to the call for aid. The Humane Society of Massachusetts awarded Captain Coombs an engraved silver pitcher for his determined lifesaving exertions.

JACHIN - *Specie Saved from Depths*

A local news brief describes the February 27, 1829, wreck of the *Jachin* from St. Martha. "The rigging and spars being capped with ice, and the crew exhausted with fatigue and cold, they were unable to work the vessel, and about half-past 8 on Thursday evening she struck on the Middle Brewster, bilged, and filled shortly after. Two of the crew, Robert Lorie and David Clark, were lost in attempting to gain the shore.

"The *Jachin* had a full cargo of fustic [a dye tree]. . .brandy, gin, and specie (the latter recovered). Captain Drew thinks the brig will be totally lost, but most of the cargo may be saved if immediately attended to and the weather proves favorable."

For twenty days the *Jachin* had been only one day's sail from Boston Harbor. The unyielding winds foiled every effort to bring the vessel in to port.

DIANA - *First Voyage Ends Abruptly*

Here is the *Boston Morning Post* report on a June 19, 1841, wreck:

> *The ship* Diana, *of Boston, Captain Boutelle, which sailed from Liverpool on the 13th of May, struck the edge of the rocks near Boston outer Light about 12 o'clock on Saturday night last. She was standing for the light with a fair, or leading, wind; and when the captain thought it prudent to haul off, he ordered the helm to be shifted in order to bring the vessel to the wind. The man at the helm misunderstood the order and hove the helm the wrong way, and there not being sufficient sea room for her to veer, she fell off by the ice and struck the rocks, her jibboom almost coming in contact with the lantern of the Light House.*

The *Diana* had thirty steerage passengers on board, but none were seriously injured. Her cargo consisted of railroad iron, salt, earthenware, and hardware. Around 420 bags of salt were thrown overboard in an attempt to refloat her. She was a new ship, not even coppered, this being her first voyage.

CARLOS - *Wrecking Vessel Survives a Blow*

A *Hingham Journal* account, dated February 7, 1851, is unusual.

> *The wrecking vessels engaged in saving cargo from the bark* Carlos, *before reported lost on Egg Rock, succeeded in saving about 100 bales of cotton, part of which has been landed at Hull. The heavy blow and severe cold weather Wednesday night and Thursday retarded the operations of the wreckers. Five of the schooners saving cargo were blown to sea, but two of them, the schooner* Ensign *of Hull and the sloop* Truth *of Boston, got into Gloucester Thursday morning with Captain Mitchell and their crews very badly frostbitten. The schooner* Albion *ashore at Hull Beach with 30 bales had not bilged as was stated, but was badly strained; she was landing her cotton.*

The *Albion* was obviously a survivor, for ten years later she was to take part in another difficult wrecking operation at Egg Rock.

Divers in cargo hold of wrecked vessel

LEWIS - *Entire Crew Perished*

Newspaper descriptions of marine disasters on January 13, 1856, include: "Portions of the cargo of the schooner reported ashore on Shag Rocks were found floating about the harbor this morning. Nothing has been found which can be identified, but she is believed to be from New York. The crew is supposed to have perished—one body has floated ashore."

A day later, we read: "The unknown vessel before reported struck on Shag Rocks in Light House Channel during the gale of Sunday morning is no doubt the packet sch. *Lewis*, Captain Crowell, from New York to Boston. She was in company in the Bay just previous to the gale with the schooner *Walcott*, Captain Bearse, from New York, which anchored on Sunday. All the crew of the *Lewis* were drowned. The shipping papers were picked up in the Bay by a fisherman, which leaves no doubt as to the fate of the vessel."

EWAN CRERAR - *Divers Engaged to Raise Cargo*

The *Ewan Crerar,* a British brig, went down on March 10, 1860. The pilot disclosed that he reached the bell buoy near the Graves and kept off, supposing he could clear the ledge. Because of a miscalculation or wind change, the vessel struck, became unmanageable, and was forced to anchor between Egg Rock and outer Brewster Island. She sank forty-five minutes later in seven fathoms, with only a few feet of her mainmast and topsail yard out of water. The rigging, sails, and spars were stripped from the brig. The crew abandoned ship, but were not in immediate danger.

The *Ewan Crerar* was bound from London, England, to Boston, and carried a load consisting of linseed oil, soda, colors, beer, whiting, steel, iron bars, horn, hide, wool, cutch (used in dyeing and tanning), antimony, and arsenic. Other assorted merchandise was on the manifest. Divers engaged to raise the cargo brought a large portion of the goods to the surface. During its early development, hard-hat diving required exceptional stamina and courage.

ENTERPRISE - *Went to Pieces on Egg Rock*

An 1861 *Merchant's Exchange Book,* one of several Boston shipping reference journals, disclosed: "The Outer Station at Hull reports that schooner *Enterprise,* of and from Nantasket for Boston, with a cargo of 150 barrels flour, 12 hogsheads molasses, struck (March 3, 1861) on Egg Rock during the squall Saturday night at half-past eight. All hands left her soon after she struck and went ashore at Boston Light. The vessel will be a total loss. Cargo will be saved in a damaged condition. She lies broadside with mastheads in water."

For the same period, *Palmer's News Room Book* revealed: "Hull, March 11–sch. *Enterprise* before reported ashore on Egg Rock, was towed off last night by schs. *Malcolm, Thetis,* and *Albion;* their lines parted soon after getting her off, and she went to pieces shortly afterwards. The wreckers succeeded in saving a portion of the hull, spars, cargo, and rigging, but were unable to recover anchor and chains."

MARITANA - *Full-rigged Ship Split in Half*

One of the most violent shipwrecks ever was that of the 991-ton *Maritana* of Providence, Rhode Island, Captain G. W. Williams, master. Built in Quincy, Massachusetts, the vessel was entering the harbor in thick weather on November 3, 1861, after sailing from Liverpool, England, with wool, coal, potash, steel, and iron. After she rammed Shag Rocks, her crew immediately cut away the masts. The bow was lodged between two huge rocks, and she took blow after blow from thundering waves. When the vessel split in half six and a half hours later, Captain Williams fell into the abyss of his ship.

A journalist wrote: "A more complete wreck was never seen. Fragments of the ship and her freight strew over all the lower islands, and occasionally a mangled body is thrown up on the jagged rocks. God save us all from a death like this."

JULIA ANNA - *Beat over Bar in Heavy Seas*

A fascinating report related a tragic wreck on January 19, 1867:

> *Captain M. B. Tower (of Hull), Underwriters Agent, went below yes-*
> *terday afternoon, and gives it as his opinion that the schooner struck*
> *on the bar between Boston Light and Great Brewster, that she immedi-*
> *ately beat over, and very soon went to pieces. There was a heavy sea*
> *rolling in at the time, and it is generally supposed that all hands per-*
> *ished. A variety of papers were picked up yesterday morning in the*
> *vicinity of Nantasket Beach, and among them a number of bills of lad-*
> *ing (flour, etc.) by the* Julia Anna.
>
> *There is one gleam of hope in regard to the crew, which is created*
> *by the fact (as reported by Mr. Pope, the agent of the Merchant's*
> *Exchange located at the outer marine station) that five men were seen*
> *at Boston Light where there are only three employed. There is a bare*
> *possibility that a portion of the crew succeeded in reaching the*
> *Lighthouse. The* Julia Anna *was a vessel of about 200 tons built at*
> *East Boston in 1852. Pieces of the hull lie strewn along the beach near*
> *the Light House.*

CHARLES H. LAWRENCE - *To Sleep Meant Death*

The *Charles H. Lawrence,* with a consignment of 926 tons of coal for the Boston and Lowell Railroad, drifted onto Outer Brewster Island during the freezing night of February 1, 1882. Expecting the schooner to be ripped apart on the rocks, the crew lowered a boat, but it was immediately smashed to pieces. Providentially, the spanker boom was thrusting over the shore, and a seventeen-year-old sailor inched along the boom over the rocks and dropped safely on land. A line then drew the dog-tired crew through the frigid surf. Captain Williams, in the custom of the sea, was the last to leave the vessel.

On this barren island with no shelter, the crew, for the rest of the grim night, exercised to keep blood circulating. The drenched captain and a few of the men strongly wished to lie down, but others urged them to stay awake; to sleep at such low temperatures meant death. A towboat picked them up the next morning.

FANNY A. PIKE - *Schooner Broke in Two*

Another lamentable wreck that took place during the February 1, 1882, gale was the *Fanny A. Pike,* belonging in Calais, Maine, and sailing from

Weehawken, New Jersey. The coal schooner drove head-on into Bald Rocks (Shag Rocks), an extremely perilous ledge. She broke in two almost immediately, with half the hull thrusting out of the sea near the ledge.

A boat launched by keeper Bates from Boston Lighthouse picked up the crew, who then transferred to a tug for conveyance to Boston. A crowd gathered on the Hull shoreline opposite Bald rocks imagined they could see two men still clinging to the wreckage, but a telescope revealed two stanchion pins jutting from the debris. Bates had been aided in the rescue by assistant keeper Bailey and Charles Pochaska, a young fisherman.

MILLIE TRIM - *Plowed into Calf Island*

A disaster on January 9, 1886, cost four lives in the wreck of the two-masted schooner *Millie Trim*, on Calf Island. The craft, of 171 tons, was launched at Bangor, Maine, in 1873 and was owned by Rockland, Maine, businessmen. She carried 265 tons of coal bound from Hoboken, New Jersey, to Boston. The *Millie Trim* plowed into rocks about 100 feet from the easterly side of the island.

The crew immediately went for the rigging, Captain Olsen reaching the main crosstrees, and the others below him. As the masts fell the captain, being higher, landed on a large boulder, but the rest of the men were lost in the breakers. Fishermen living on Calf Island saved Captain Olsen by rowing to his aid in a small dory, a courageous act in turbulent surf that was witnessed from the signal station on Telegraph Hill in Hull. The telegraph operators notified Boston officials of the incident and additional help was dispatched.

LOUISA SMITH - *Capsized When Cargo Shifted*

During a heavy southeast gale on October 18, 1890, the *Louisa Smith* sank in Broad Sound, two miles north-northwest of the Graves Ledge whistling buoy. The captain advised that the vessel encountered the gale when working into Massachusetts Bay, and when off the Graves the craft lurched suddenly, shifting the cargo of 1,600 barrels of cement. She capsized, quickly filled, and slid beneath the wind-whipped waters almost immediately. The fishing schooner *Sarah C. Whorf* made a timely appearance and picked up the crew just as the heavily laden vessel sank.

The *Louisa Smith* hailed from Thomaston, Maine, under Captain Matthews from Eddyville, with cargo consigned to the Boston firm of Waldo Brothers. She was a two-masted schooner of 137 tons, built in Brookville, Maine, in 1868 and owned by E. K. O'Brien of Thomaston. The craft was last reported lying in Lighthouse Channel with topmasts jutting about five feet above the surface.

ELMER E. RANDALL - *Collision Near Boston Lightship*

Captain E. S. Hopkins of the two-master *Elmer E. Randall,* who lost his vessel on July 20, 1897, explained:

> *We were bound in from a fishing trip with about 26,000 pounds of cod. Approaching the lightship during a dense fog, the three masts of a schooner were seen bearing down upon us, and although we sounded our fog horn to notify those on the schooner of our close proximity the vessel soon struck us, and in from five to ten minutes my schooner plunged forward and went down in eleven fathoms of water. The 14 members of the crew and myself had time to save absolutely nothing, and most of us are without the necessary means of defraying our expenses to our homes.*

The schooner was built at Essex, Massachusetts, in 1893, and registered 56.91 gross tons, and 54.13 net tons. She was 73.2 feet long, with 20-foot beam, and 71.6 feet depth of hold. No insurance was carried on the vessel. Captain Hopkins further indicated that the *"Elmer E. Randall* had the right of way and the matter would be settled in the courts."

CALVIN F. BAKER - *On Wrong Side of Lighthouse*

A terrible wreck in the November 27, 1898, tempest left the schooner *Calvin F. Baker* on a ledge about seventy-five yards behind Boston Lighthouse. Running for port in the blinding snow, the craft entered the harbor on the wrong side of the lighthouse. A viewer from Nantasket commented: "Nothing but the blackened hull can be seen above the wash of the surf and she looks like an old hulk that had found a bed there years ago." Several sailors were drawn into the frothing waves.

The surviving crew were rescued when the Humane Society surfboat *Boston Herald* appeared and lifesavers cut them from their lashings in the rigging. The steward was found frozen to death in the icy shrouds. Observers pointed out that the surfmen were forced to row across almost three miles of tumbling sea to reach the lee side. The vessel, owned in Boston, had a cargo of coal. The tide on this occasion was higher than any since the 1851 storm, in which the first Minot's Lighthouse, off Cohasset, Massachusetts, was destroyed.

KEYSTONE - *Old Schooner-Barge Wrecked*

On February 25, 1900, the tug *Gettysburg,* towing the coal schooner-barges *Otto* and *Keystone,* was shortening up the towline while off Boston Light. A brisk wind was blowing from the south-southwest, and a strong undertow was flowing. Before the tug could pick up headway the schooners struck at Shag Rocks, and both were in danger of breaking up.

The five-man crew of the *Otto* and the four aboard the *Keystone* were rescued and temporarily treated at Boston Light. The *Otto* managed to work free, though severely disabled; the *Keystone* was a complete loss. The mariners were later provided with dry clothing by the Women's National Relief Association while lodged at the U.S. Life Saving Station in Hull. The *Keystone* was an old schooner and carried 1,258 tons of coal valued at around $5,000.

COLUMBIA - *Sank in Lighthouse Channel*

The fishing schooner *Columbia* sank in Lighthouse Channel on October 7, 1901, an hour after striking the dreaded Graves Ledge. The vessel, under Captain Jessie Thomas, and nine men, had about 25,000 pounds of cod, haddock, and hake from the fishing grounds off Cape Elizabeth. Despite the crew's endeavors the water gained through a sizable hole stove in her hull. All hands had barely jumped into the dories when she settled to the bottom. The schooner went down near Point Allerton in six fathoms, abreast of Nash's Rock buoy, but, being just off the southern side of the channel, created no hazard to navigation.

The *Columbia* was constructed at Newburyport, Massachusetts, in 1894, and worked out of Boston from T Wharf. She was 61.5 feet long, 17.5 feet in the beam, drew 7.5 feet, and weighed 40 gross tons. The vessel was owned by Captain Jessie L. Scott of Boston.

KIOWA - *Divers Work on Steamer*

Quantities of cargo from the steamer *Kiowa* washed ashore at Hull and Cohasset following the fierce storm of January 3, 1904. The beaches were lined with people waiting to gather up crates of oranges, bales of cotton, and hard pine. The manifest also included pineapples, cottonseed meal, rosin, turpentine, rice, clay, iron cores, and other general merchandise. The steamer had been struck by the freighter *Admiral Dewey* on December 29, 1903, with such force that she was cut through the plates below the waterline almost to the keel. The crew were forced to leave when the water rose to waist level and the boiler fires went out. When the remaining bulkheads suddenly burst under tons of pressure, the *Kiowa* plummeted to the bottom.

Divers worked diligently on the wreck, but even under the best conditions progress was slow. The site is recorded as on the southerly side of the channel, a short mile from Boston Light, and almost in a direct line between the black buoy off Point Allerton and that marking Ultonia Ledge.

CHROMO - *Cleaved in Two by Steamer*

In a "dungeon" fog on July 3, 1905, the huge steamer *Calvin Austin,* carrying several hundred passengers, cut in two the little two-masted schooner *Chromo,* roughly a mile southeast of Boston Light. The prow of the steamer cut off the schooner's stern. In less than ten minutes the smaller vessel had filled and was on her way to a deep grave.

The impenetrable fog made rescue exceptionally difficult, and survivors prayed that they would be quickly picked up. All but one man, who could not be found, were hauled aboard the steamer, which then continued on its voyage to St. John, Nova Scotia. The *Chromo* was employed in the fishing industry, but at the time of the accident was in ballast and being put through her paces for several prospective buyers. At times the vessel, owned by a Boston-based wrecking company, had been used for salvage.

C. H. LANE - *Observant Woman Merits Praise*

The *Boston Post* carried a story about a March 20, 1906, wreck:

> *Plunging into what seemed the jaws of death, two courageous assistant lightkeepers at Boston Light, Charles W. Jordan and H. C. Tolle, rode the mountainous waves in Monday night's raging gale in a frail 14-foot Swampscott dory, and at the risk of being swept to sea, managed, after great difficulty, to effect the rescue of the entire crew of six of the stranded three-masted clay-laden schooner* C. H. Lane, *which went ashore on the southwestern side of Brewster Island, on which the light is situated.*

The men in the lighthouse, as well as those rescued, heartily praised Mrs. Nellie Jordan, wife of the first assistant lightkeeper, who, from the lighthouse tower, first saw the distress signal on the schooner. Had it not been for her watchfulness, the men's peril probably would not have been discovered in time for those in the lighthouse to go after them.

MARY LEE NEWTON - *Ten Hours atop Cabin*

The *Boston Globe* vividly recounted a sailing craft's sinking on November 15, 1906.

Standing for 10 hours on top of the cabin of their little schooner, the Mary Lee Newton, *coal laden, bound for Eastport, Me., wondering whether the next sea would sweep them away, was the hardship endured by Captain E. M. Aylward of Melrose, mate D. W. Preston, cook Howard Titus, and seaman Emerson Harvey last night when the vessel ran ashore on False Spit Bar, between Bug and Boston lights, down the harbor. The vessel will probably be a total loss, but some of the gear, such as anchors, windlass, etc., will be saved. The captain and his crew saved nothing but what they had on. At 6 o'clock this morning they were rescued by the lifesaving crew at Hull.*

Captain Aylward expressed the gale's wildness: "The vessel before going ashore had been thrown about as if it were a dory."

A. HEATON - *Foundered with Lime Afire*

News in the *Boston Post* highlighted the end of the *A. Heaton* on January 24, 1907. "With her mainmast torn away by the wind, huge holes in her bottom caused by pounding on Outer Brewster, and her cargo of lime afire, the two-masted schooner *A. Heaton* foundered about 4 o'clock yesterday morning at the very entrance to Boston Harbor, near Thieves Ledge, and her crew of five nearly perished with cold before they reached Boston Light in an open boat."

Before striking the rock, Captain Hart and Seaman James Coffin stationed themselves at the wheel and were lashed to the stanchions to avoid being washed overboard. Ice soon covered oilskins and lashings, binding them to their place of duty. The lookouts heard the roar of waves breaking over the ledge just off the island and yelled a warning, and almost immediately struck three times, soon sliding off into deep water. The entire crew were fortunate in abandoning ship before the end.

HUGH G. - *Five Drown near Graves Ledge*

At midnight on November 21, 1908, the British schooner *Hugh G.*, with tons of rock plaster in her holds, was sunk half a mile northwest of Graves Ledge by collision with a mud scow towed by the tug *Minot J. Wilcox*. After hearing accounts from the three survivors, who were in the numbing sea fully ten minutes, a newsman wrote:

Then began a struggle for life. Some of the men seized fragments of deck fittings that floated up from the wreck, They swam about shouting for help. The tug was some distance away and it seemed ages to the men before she turned about. By the time the tug came near them the five men had gone down, unable to continue the unequal fight. The survivors were chilled to the marrow by the icy waters and they were nearly exhausted when dragged aboard the Wilcox. *One of the men was unconscious and it was some time before he was resuscitated. The others were in a precarious condition and it required several hours' attention to restore them.*

A yawl in which the crew attempted to abandon ship was sucked down in a whirlpool caused by the sinking wreck. The schooner settled in sixty feet of water. A U.S. Revenue Service cutter was dispatched to pull out her masts, eliminating any danger of collision.

JOHN J. FALLON - *Night of Terror in Gale*

The Boston fishing schooner *John J. Fallon* went down in four fathoms on January 1, 1914, with 45,000 pounds of bottom fish and 2,000 pounds of halibut. The vessel was running into port following the first trip under a new skipper. She stood too far to the north after passing Bug Light and ran on the rocks just inside Kelley's Ledge at False Spit. Heavy seas endlessly struck her while the mariners spent a night of terror in the gale. Finally, when dawn broke, the schooner was discovered by a lookout with the Stony Beach lifesavers.

A tug, and the wrecking lighter *Salvor,* were trying to pull the craft off the rocks, but the immense strain forced the keel from the hull and she started to fill. The crew of twenty-three were barely able to grab a few personal belongings and scramble to the *Salvor.* News clippings pointed out that the *John J. Fallon* was the third fishing schooner in three days to strike in the outer harbor.

ANNIE PERRY - *Cut into Her Side like a Knife*

The schooner Annie Perry *was creeping in from a nine-day trip to the Banks with a fare of 30,000 pounds groundfish. The steam trawler* Surf *had left the pier just before midnight by the South Channel for the fishing grounds. It was at a point a mile outside Boston Light that the two boats drew together without warning through the dead wall of night. The men and officers agree that one could hardly see a vessel's length, and that made it impossible for the lookouts in either craft to see the other in turn. There was no chance to avoid the crash.*

All in a moment there was the faint gleam of the vessel's lights through the haze, a creak as their wheels were jammed hard over and the grinding of timbers as the trawler's bow struck the Annie Perry *just abaft the fore rigging and cut into her side like a knife.*

This October 20, 1914, news item shows how quickly disaster can strike. The crew at least were promptly picked up; they would sail another day.

ROMANCE - *Sank As It Burst into Flame*

The *Boston Daily Globe* reported on the *Romance,* destroyed September 9, 1936. "In a dense, treacherous fog which hung all day over Boston Harbor, the *S.S. New York,* bound from Boston to New York, at 7:05 last night crashed just forward amidships into the excursion steamer *Romance,* on her daily trip from Provincetown to Boston, off Graves Light buoy, Boston Harbor. The *Romance,* almost cut in half, sank within 20 minutes, just as it was bursting into flames."

The *New York* let down ladders to the deck of the *Romance* as the steamer was lowering her lifeboats. All 153 passengers and crew of 59 were taken off, and shortly thereafter she went down in a cloud of steam. The *Romance* skipper, Adelbert C. Wickens, searched every compartment and, following tradition, was the last to abandon ship; a nonswimmer, he kicked away from the vessel as it sank. The pilothouse floated off and was salvaged by Nahant wreckers. Army engineers advised that the wreck was in seventy-five feet of water, one-half mile west-northwest of Graves lighted whistle buoy 1A.

CITY OF SALISBURY - *The Famed Zoo Ship*

On April 22, 1938, the *City of Salisbury,* loaded with an unusual cargo of wild animals, reptiles, exotic birds, and valuable general merchandise, steamed toward the fogged-in harbor. The 419-foot freighter, well off course, ran onto a spire of rocks a short distance from Graves Lighthouse. The vessel wedged itself into the reef, making it mandatory to remove the menagerie and much of the cargo. Most of the animals were brought safely to shore. The accident broke the freighter's back, and attempts to tow her off to a dry dock were abandoned.

An observer recorded the fatal moments: "Ominous groans of tearing steel plates echoed throughout the ship as the swells tipped the ship back and forth like a pendulum." Later in the fall (1938), a second storm hit the coast and the zoo ship rolled over and settled further into her last berth. Even to this day, bales of natural rubber from the cargo occasionally pop to the surface. The uncharted rock became known as Salisbury Pinnacle.

Stately passenger steamer Romance *went down in Broad Sound.*
(Courtesy: Peabody Museum of Salem)

City of Salisbury *broken in half near Graves Light* **(Courtesy: Peabody Museum of Salem)**

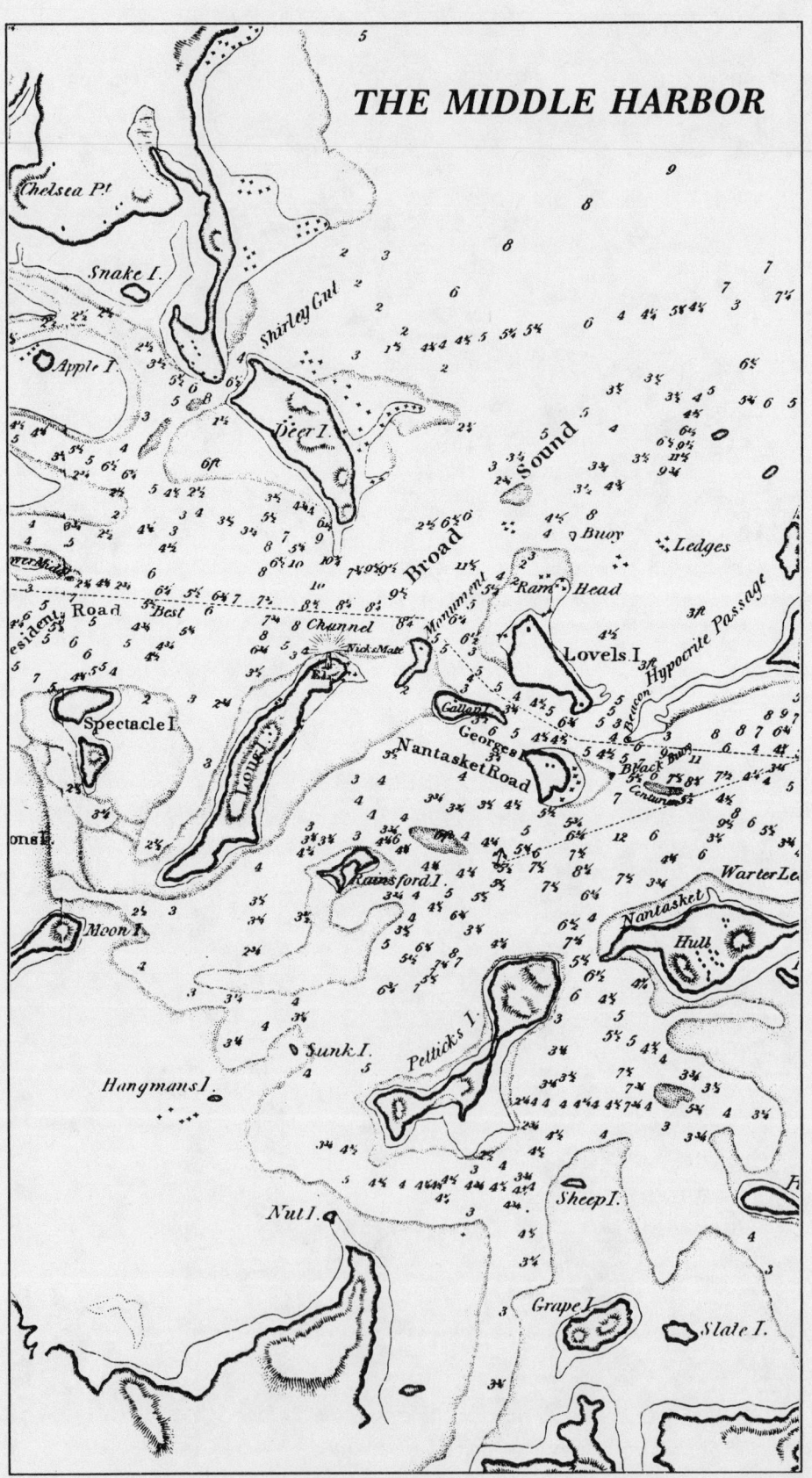

THE MIDDLE HARBOR

The Middle Harbor

⚏

Middle-Islands Shipwrecks

Deer, Gallop's, Lovell's, and Georges Island are considered the middle-islands cluster.

Deer Island, at the harbor's northern opening, was once separated from Point Shirley, Winthrop, by Shirley Gut, a swift-flowing ship channel. The island was the domain of the Indian sachem Winnepurkitt, the hero in a John Greenleaf Whittier poem. Sadly, Chief Winnepurkitt, like many other native Americans, was sold into slavery in the West Indies. Many Indians were shipped to North Africa to suffer and perish in unaccustomed heat. Might the same vessels have returned with black Africans who were to toil on lands the Indian once walked? Some eminent Bostonians were not averse to turning a tainted dollar in the slave trade.

At the height of King Philip's War, the colonists interred several hundred Christian Indians on Deer Island during the harsh winter of 1675–76. Some died on the island from exposure or malnutrition, and legend relates that their spirits still roam the desolate shores.

A local pirate is supposed to have buried his treasure around Point Shirley, or, as others contend, on a nearby island. Although some of the loot allegedly has been discovered, gems, including a priceless diamond, have escaped detection. Another claim is that part of Captain Kidd's fortune was unearthed close by at Winthrop Head. Like most treasure-trove rumors, the tales are hazy and hazard the reputation of the teller who repeats them. In the late 1600s this island was designated the harbor quarantine station, perhaps prompting sea rovers to secrete their riches elsewhere.

A naval battle began at the westerly end of the Gut on May 19, 1776, when the American privateer *Franklin* stranded. The British force attacked in whaleboats, two of them being sunk by cannon fire before the rising tide allowed the *Franklin* to escape. The American commander, James Mugford, lost his life in the encounter, a story that might reward research by a military historian.

William Tewksbury, a well-known rescuer residing on the island, wrote in correspondence: "In 1800, I saved John Calef of York from the masthead of his schooner, which was sunk on Fawn Bar. Black Sam, who assisted me, has since drowned in the Gut."

In the War of 1812, the forty-four-gun frigate *Constitution*, "Old Ironsides," used Shirley Gut to avoid the foe's naval blockade of Boston Harbor.

Frigate Constitution *in dry dock at Charlestown Navy Yard*
(Courtesy: Peabody Museum of Salem)

A Massachusetts Humane Society lifeboat station was placed on the eastern slope of the central hill. A 1933 storm substantially filled in Shirley Gut with rock and sand, so that prisoners interred on the island's House of Industry who were inclined to escape were no longer terrorized by the current. At one time the rush of water through the channel was so strong that boats had to be hauled through with lines brought ashore.

The prisoners helped remove general cargo from the schooner *A. H. Brooks* (sailing to Maine), and molasses, potash, and wool from the *George Brooks* (sailing from Maine), also a schooner. The vessels were wrecked at the island almost in the same place during gales on November 26, 1888, and November 26, 1898, respectively.

Mountainous waves had tossed the beached coaster *A. H. Brooks* higher on the eastern shore than any other vessel in the island's history. Fifty prisoners unloaded corn, grain, hay, meal, potatoes, straw, furniture, and oil from the schooner. The surprised prisoners noticed not only navigational instruments and other valuables in the captain's cabin, but leftovers from a partially finished meal; the crew, however, was nowhere to be found.

Another Maine schooner, also named *George Brooks,* carrying molasses and potash, went ashore at Deer Island in the December 8, 1842 snowstorm. The cargo was carted across the island to the lee side and loaded on another schooner.

The crest of the hill on the island became a Harbor Entrance Control Post during World War II. The U.S. Navy operated signal devices, radar, and the antisubmarine net from there. The naval forces stationed vessels at the net's entrance and logged ships in and out through the narrow gate. A battery of sixteen-inch guns (battleship size) were assigned to Fort Dawes, an Army post named to honor Revolutionary War patriot William Dawes.

In *Battle of Boston Harbor,* John H. Fenton tells the wartime history of U.S. Coast Guard Reserve Flotilla 1-412, including a potentially serious mission that ended with a humorous incident:

> *It was dark in the early evening of 19 March 1944. The radio watch on Boston Lifeboat Station picked up the shore telephone and heard a tense voice from Harbor Entrance Control Point announcing that a strange and unidentified object was in the main channel about 200 yards beyond the submarine net. There had been some submarine activity off the Atlantic coast within the month. Bravely, the crew of the* CG 38520, *a picket boat, set out to investigate.*
>
> *They returned in a short time and fears at HECP were set at rest. The object was a waterlogged Christmas tree, floating base upward out to sea. . . .*
>
> *One day in July 1943, however, a fishing vessel came through the*

net with an unexploded anti-submarine bomb aboard. The bomb had been dragged up with a load of fish, about 25 miles southeast of Boston, Gingerly, the bomb was handed into the gig from BLBS and taken to the station. More sighs of relief.

During World War II, an identified German U-boat reportedly had sowed several mines off the outer harbor; the *1-412* crew had cause for apprehension.

Deer Island Light, an ironclad beacon, formerly stood on the end of a spit about a quarter-mile off the southern tip.

Gallop's Island, farther into the harbor, at one time was owned by the first Boston Harbor pilot, John Gallop, who was officially appointed by the government to safely guide vessels through the tortuous channels.

The island's northern bluff held military earthworks erected by French engineers during the Revolutionary War. It was also known for its fertile produce gardens and a reliable spring, which were a godsend for mariners quarantined in the nearby Hospital Roads anchorage. A red flag fluttered from the masthead of a quarantined vessel when her crew mustered for inspection by the port physician.

The island's owners also sold ballast to ship captains, but countless tons of gravel from Gallop's and nearby Nix's Mate have been washed into the Narrows and adjoining channels by gnawing storms and currents.

Gallop's Island passed from military to civilian rule as the wars came and went. In the late 1800s it was designated a quarantine station, and there more than two hundred smallpox victims repose. Also, it was a colony for a few isolated cases of leprosy.

The island forms the northern barrier of the Narrows, one of the most critical harbor ship passages to protect in wartime. In a shaft reportedly tun-

Deer Island Light

Deer Island Hospital, Boston Harbor

neled beneath the Narrows from Gallop's to Lovell's Island, explosives could be detonated under enemy ships steaming through the channel. Several thousand Civil War recruits trained here. Tragically, during the 1888 storm, coffins in the island graveyard were washed out by waves, strewing bones of buried soldiers along the beach.

On August 10, 1928, the *Nantasket*, of the Nantasket Steamboat Company, and the fishing schooner *Isabella*, collided in fog, and both were beached on Gallop's Island. The steamer, which carried no passengers, was left high and dry beside the schooner when the tide receded.

German sailors, after sabotaging their own docked merchant vessels when World War I erupted, were interred on Gallop's. The island served too as a Maritime Service Radio and Seamanship School under U.S. Coast Guard instructors.

Nix's Mate is the name given to the dry part of the extensive shoal that runs from the northwest of Gallop's for several hundred yards to the north. Its twelve acres of land were popular with skippers because of the ballast-size stones scattered over the shore. These stones could be picked up by a mariner, placed in a wheelbarrow, and wheeled up a plank onto a vessel.

In the 1888 *Bowen's Picture of Boston*, the author depicts Nix's Mate:

> There is a beacon of split rock, in the centre nearly 40 feet square, fastened together by copper bolts, which perfectly secures it from the tremendous force of the waves in times of northeasterly gales. To speak more

definitely, the shape is a parallelogram, the sides being 12 feet high, and ascended by stone steps in the south side. On the top of this is a six-sided pyramid of wood 20 feet high, with one window on the south. This is the conspicuous part of the beacon, and serves as a prominent warning to seamen to keep from the dangerous shoal on which it stands.

Early French traders might have named the site Niches Mate to indicate the concavity, or niche, between the islet and Gallop's Island, through which vessels could pass. It is so named on an early English map which reads: "The pricked line [between Gallop's Island and Niches Mate] is the ship's channel."

Some claim that the former wooden beacon, painted a somber black, looked much like a gibbet at a distance, in keeping with the tradition that ancient pirate hangings were done here. Another popular, but questionable, story tells of a murdered Captain Nix, whose first mate was allegedly hanged on the islet for the deed. But admiralty law set strict standards for recording any such trial or execution, and no documentation appears in Boston or other court files. Another, probably apocryphal, variation is that a pirate called Nix buried a treasure and his potentially talkative first mate on that bit of earth.

Another ancient account is that a passenger on the *Jewel*, a vessel that Governor Winthrop owned, asked a Dutch pilot about the island. At the time, the sea breaking on the shore was causing unearthly sounds. The pilot responded by identifying the place as "Nixie Shmalt" (phonetically spelled), which translated reportedly meant "wail of the water spirits."

The pride of the Boston fishing fleet, the *Bay State*, a 124-foot trawler carrying 80,000 pounds of groundfish, ran high and dry onto the shoal

Nix's Mate, Boston Harbor

in 1967, causing embarrassment to her crew and disrupting scheduled fish sales.

On the northeast perimeter of the Narrows is Lovell's Island, which with Man-o'-war and Ram Head bars, has proven a great detriment to navigation. This island, close to the center of the harbor, has been surrounded by Boston maritime history. The island's shape, some say, was altered by the 1782 wreck of the French seventy-four-gun warship *Magnifique,* a leviathan that lies on Man-o'-war Bar (also called Seventy-four Bar) to the west of the northern end of Lovell's.

A 1794 *Topographical and Historical Description of Boston,* published in Massachusetts Historical Society Collections, revealed two huts-of-refuge strategically positioned on the island. Here, the first lifesaving facility in America was built, after a wreck in which the passengers froze to death. One hut was "on the N.E. side, on ground about forty rods from the shore; the other on the S.E. point, near to the Black Rocks. . . . Poles are erected on these huts with balls painted white, as marks where they stand. They are furnished with the necessities for the comfort and relief of the unfortunate who come on the coast. He must be an unfeeling wretch who robs them of any necessities which they contain."

A U.S. Lighthouse Service buoy station was erected on Lovell's in 1874. Range lights once stood on the northeast side, one at latitude 42° 19' 58", longitude 70° 55' 49", and the second at 215 1/4°, 134 yards to the rear of the first. The illumination was rated at 490 and 840 candle-power, respectively. Treasure was allegedly discovered within a stone's throw of the beacons.

Fort Standish, named for Pilgrim soldier Myles Standish, began operat-

The Old Range Lights, Boston Harbor

ing in 1900. The massive bastion protected several batteries of heavy coast-defense guns, including ten-inch-bore rifles.

Directly south of Lovell's lies Georges Island, always a keystone in the harbor defenses. The first fort of any significance on the island went up during the War of Independence. French marines and sailors dug in to cover any approach to their anchored fleet, which shortly before had been battered by storms and English cannon off the coast.

The 1777 Report of the Committee on the Fortification of Boston Harbor recommended sinking hulks in the channel at the back of Georges to block men-o'-war. Enemy ships would have to pass nearly a quarter-mile closer to the batteries at Hull, keeping them in range longer.

As he arrived in Boston Harbor aboard the ship *Alert* in 1836, Richard Henry Dana, Jr., author of *Two Years Before the Mast,* looked down from the royal yard: "So close is the channel to some of these islands that we ran the end of our flying jibboom over some of the outwork of the fortifications of Georges Island, and had the opportunity of seeing the advantage of that point as a fortified place; for in working up the channel, we presented a fair stem and stern for raking from the batteries three or four times. One gun might have knocked us to pieces."

An 1840s analyst mentioned the severe damage a gale had done to the huge granite seawall blocks, held together with thick iron bars: "It appears that no power under Heaven could move them, and yet there is at times a fearful, terrible unaccountable force of the sea, a force that makes us feel our own feebleness, and instinctively leads us to build our hopes and safety on Him who controls the whirlwind and directs the storms, rather than upon granite and iron, though to all appearances as strong and adamant, and indissolubly bound together."

The pentagonal exterior of Fort Warren still looks as formidable as in the Civil War era. Military architect Sylvanus Thayer, father of West Point, based Fort Warren's design on the French star shape to repel any assault with interlacing fire. Rebel prisoners, including the vice-president of the Confederacy, were interred within the dark labyrinths. Officers of the Confederate warships *Tacony* and *Atlanta* attempted several daring escapes, one of which ended off the Maine coast when they were captured under the guns of the U.S. Revenue cutter *Dobbin.*

One prisoner's spouse was so intent on rescuing her loved one that she allegedly landed on the island with a small boat and reached her husband. When the escape party was discovered, she raised a pistol to fire at the fort's commandant, Colonel Dimmick. She fired, the old weapon blew apart, and a fragment killed her husband. The story that Colonel Dimmick ordered that the woman be executed is unsubstantiated. You can

View of Fort Warren Boston harbor.

Interior of the Fort.

read details about the Lady in Black, whose spirit is said to roam the ramparts still, in Edward Rowe Snow's writings.

In the late 1800s, Fort Warren had 300 guns and about 1,500 troops. It had some large, some small parts in all American conflicts until World War II. During that war, the fort was a control center for mines that would be exploded under enemy warships. The harbor was, of course, heavily mined and fenced off with torpedo nets, and masters and pilots of vessels navigating there were thoroughly warned about how to stay clear of the defenses.

Georges has had its share of violent shipwrecks, including the ship *John* on November 3, 1703. She had sailed from Lisbon, Portugal, carrying wine and salt. *America*, a fishing craft, is briefly mentioned as going to pieces on April 23, 1833.

Apparently the tale is true that a German submarine activated a magnetic detection cable off the outer harbor in 1942, while sowing bottom mines. Naval minesweepers frequently swept critical sectors all during the war, but they found no explosive devices. The German sub that laid the mines, the *U-67,* was lost with all hands off Portugal about a year later.

The United States minesweeper *YMS-14* went down in the North Channel of Broad Sound after colliding with a destroyer *(DD-638)* on January 11, 1945. *YMS-14*'s armament consisted of a three-inch antiaircraft gun, four 50-caliber machine guns, two single-depth charge throwers, and eight 300-pound depth charges. She was blown up with 750 pounds of explosives as a navigational menace.

In another naval incident, the patrol boat *Alacrity* was temporarily stranded upon ice near Boston Light in February 1918.

During the war years, news about military vessels was often restricted, or kept vague, to deny intelligence to the enemy. A typical wreck account read: AN ATLANTIC PORT, Feb. 4—A coastwise steamer which was caught in a heavy ice field off the New England Coast yesterday was unable to extricate herself today, but is expected to proceed tomorrow. Government vessels sent to her assistance returned today and reported that the steamer was not damaged to any extent and was in no danger."

Wreck statistics emphatically unveil the harbor's pitfalls.

UNIDENTIFIED - *Cargo Included Silver*

On November 28, 1682, a gale accompanied by thick snow enveloped an unidentified brig of about 100 tons approaching the harbor. Sailing from the West Indies the vessel had a general cargo, which reportedly included silver. She may have first struck an offshore shoal somewhere between Faun Bar (also known as Fawn Bar), Deer Island, and Winthrop Bar. The vessel stranded about a quarter-mile north of Pullen Point Gut. A few sailors were carried overboard in the surf that swept the deck. Ten mariners, including a Captain Horton, were able to reach shore, but four faltered and froze to death.

The account is verified by a relative of Governor Winthrop, in whose residence shelter and sustenance were provided. The value, or weight, of the silver was not fully disclosed; however, it could well have been mainly in bar, sphere, or plate form rather than coin. After it is exposed to oxidation by salt water, silver is blackened.

MAGNIFIQUE - *Harbor's Most Historic Wreck*

The historic French seventy-four gun *Magnifique* was wrecked while entering Boston Harbor on August 15, 1782. Often confused with the unsubstantiated loss of a British pay ship, the *Magnifique,* launched at Brest on March 18, 1749, was rated first class. She was 170 feet long, and fully manned with a crew of 750 men. Serving as a flagship on several occasions, she distinguished herself in combat against the British. During 1782, the *Magnifique* was in the Marquis of Vaudreuil's squadron, commanded by Captain Macteigne.

Boston Harbor pilot David Darling, blamed for the towering man-o'-war's wreck was reduced to sexton and undertaker at New North Church. Bostonians treated him as a pariah for the embarrassing incident, and children would scribble on the church door, "Don't send this ship ashore, as you did the 74." Darling has been castigated by historians over the centuries for his poor navigation, and one famed chronicler indicated that French sailors died because the wreck was so disastrous.

The captain's official letters, however, reveal that a sudden shift in wind and tardy reaction by the crew caused the ship to ground on a shoal off the northwest end of Lovell's Island. No evidence whatsoever suggests that pilot Darling was off course. Further, the *Magnifique* came to rest on the bar without even shaking. She did not plow into bristling rocks, tearing out her bottom and then sliding into the depths forever, as some contemporary writers would have us believe. She stranded about an hour before low tide just where other French warships occasionally grounded without mishap. By the next high tide, though, the aging *Magnifique* had filled, and her decks were under harbor waters.

The French sailors and marines had to abandon ship, and saving her cannon (thirty thirty-six pounders, thirty eighteen-pounders, fourteen eight-pounders) became the salvagers' mission. Efforts to refloat the ship seem not to have been especially energetic. Some bureaucrats promptly decided that our nation should compensate France for the *Magnifique,* and offered the new *America,* also a seventy-four, then on the stocks at Portsmouth, New Hampshire. Darling clearly was mocked because many saw the offer both as a blow to their patriotic pride and as a drain on the fledgling nation's pocketbook.

Captain John Paul Jones, greatest naval hero of the times, had supervised building of the *America,* which was to be the first seventy-four-gun ship in our arsenal and under his command. So disillusioned was he at losing his vessel that he resigned his commission and sailed off with the French fleet when it left Boston Harbor. The *Magnifique* wreck's ramifications were far-reaching and tainted with political intrigue.

The *America,* commanded by Captain Macteigne, formerly of the *Magnifique,* eventually sailed, armed with the latter's cannon. Most historians assert that the *America* was captured by the British. The original *America,* however, was scrapped at Brest, and a second, French-constructed vessel of the same name was the actual casualty. It is even said that the British Admiralty assumed they had taken the Portsmouth-built ship.

Antiquarians generally believe that the lost *Magnifique* is now beneath the dry part of Lovell's Island. Although the shoal named Seventy-four Bar seems to have formed over the hulk, bearings taken to the wreck site indicate no radical topographical change since the mid-1800s, when she was last seen. At that time, cannon balls and other artifacts were recovered.

LUCRETIA - *Snowstorm Cloaked the Sea*

A blinding snowstorm smothered visibility on December 4, 1786, and was responsible for the wreck of the brig *Lucretia,* which bilged off Deer Island near Point Shirley. The vessel carried a consignment of coffee from St. Croix, Virgin Islands. Her home port was New Haven, Connecticut. Captain Powell and five hands remained on board, preserving their lives close to the still-burning ship's stove. Five other mariners, including Mr. Kilby, the mate, and Mr. Sharp, a Boston merchant, reached shore but succumbed to the intense cold.

Sharp's funeral was held at the American Coffee House on State Street, and was well attended by fellow Boston businessmen. The brig was owned by Messrs. Bolling and Sharp.

UNIDENTIFIED BRIG - *Couple Locked in Frozen Embrace*

On December 10, 1786, another snowstorm caused the destruction of an unidentified brig sailing from Damariscotta, Maine, to Boston. At about midnight the craft, commanded by a John Askins, was forced onto Ram Head, a bar extending off the northerly part of Lovell's Island. All thirteen persons landed safely despite chilling winds that increased and sent the mercury below zero. All sought refuge on the lee side of a huge glacial boulder.

During a morning search for survivors, a resident of Georges Island discovered the poor souls huddled together, but none stirred. Among them was a young couple who were anticipating marriage; they were locked in a frozen embrace. The boulder has since been known as Lover's Rock, from the heart-rending drama more than two centuries ago.

MIDAS - *Carried Substantial Sum of Specie*

The *Salem Gazette* mentions a significant sum of money that was lost on January 17, 1820: "The brig *Midas,* of Newburyport, from St. Domingo, bound to Boston, while lying to for a pilot off Boston Light, was run afoul by another vessel, and sank; the crew except one man being saved by the pilot boat—the fate of the other vessel not known; $10,000 dollars in specie was said to be on board."

The newspaper also revealed: "Confirmation [of the article above] from Merchant's Hall, brig *Midas,* Varina [the captain] of Newburyport, 31 days from City of St. Domingo for Boston, with a cargo of mahogany, lignum vitae, molasses, logwood, coffee, and specie. The *Midas* sank in about 8 minutes, crew saved, with nothing but what they had on, by the pilot boat *Hornet.*" (The wreck was located in five fathoms, not far from Georges Island.)

ELIZABETH & ANN - *All on Board Presumed Lost*

The *Boston Daily Advertiser Marine Journal* reported a vessel wrecked on March 5, 1829.

> *Captain Tewksbury, who came up to town on Friday afternoon from Point Shirley, has reported at Merchants Hall that pieces of the hull and some oranges and cigars, being part of the cargo of the brig* Elizabeth & Ann, *Wm. H. Savage, came ashore at Deer Island on Thursday night.*
>
> *Captain T. presumes that the vessel struck on Winthrop's Bar in the gale on Thursday night, and probably every person on board was lost. The quarter deck came ashore at Cedar Point, and the bottom is at the north part of the Island near Fawn Bar.*

The brig's manifest listed coffee, sweetmeats, cigars, molasses, and oranges.

TRIO - *Frothing Sea Prevented Rescue*

The brig *Trio,* Captain John Humphrey commanding, out of Portland, Maine, sixty-three days from Havana, Cuba, with 400 hogsheads and 39 tierces of molasses, went ashore on February 20, 1837, at Deer Island. She was making for Boston Light as a dense snowstorm commenced. Because the crew was all but exhausted after a long voyage, Captain Humphrey felt obliged to run for port, but the *Trio* struck on Faun Bar, tore off her rudder, and beat over. Both anchors were let go, but about an hour later, at midnight, she dragged onto the beach.

All hands tied themselves to the wreck but by 8 o'clock next morning she broke in two. The vessel soon went completely to pieces, one chunk carrying the young mate ashore. The officer last observed his father, the captain, hung up in the rudder hole, where the unfortunate man drowned.

NUN - *Limer Burned to Water's Edge*

On September 25, 1847, the schooner *Nun* from Thomaston, Maine, went ashore on Gallop's Island with a load of lime. The material ignited and the vessel burned to the waterline.

The greatest danger to craft carrying lime was a leaking hull, for water, air, and lime had to be kept apart or fire would result. Platforms were constructed in the hold to keep the lime casks above any bilge water. A smoldering fire in a limer was fairly common.

All portholes, hatches, and the cabin were painstakingly sealed to smother any uncontrollable combustion; the crew therefore had to live on the bare decks. If the fire were not extinguished, the vessel's hull would start to blister as temperature in the cargo hold rose. Scuttling in shallow water was the only way of ending such an ordeal, and complete submersion would sometimes save the vessel.

OCEAN - *Stoves Apparently Tipped over*

The steamer *Ocean* left her berth in Boston on November 25, 1854, headed for the Kennebec River, Maine, with about eighty passengers. Approaching the Lower Middle, roughly half a mile south of Deer Island, she was rammed by the British steamship *Canada*. She was struck abaft the larboard (port) wheelhouse, ripping her down to the waterline. Apparently the stoves tipped over in the collision, and the *Ocean* caught fire immediately. Craft in the area sent boats to her assistance, but several lives were lost.

The *Ocean*'s engine continued to function, and she was run ashore at Deer Island, a quarter-mile south of the hospital. The fire persisted for a few hours, however, and she burned to the waterline. The incident was attributed to the four steamers' belonging to the Eastern Line (*Boston, Forest City, Eastern State,* and *Ocean*) being close together while outward bound, when they unexpectedly met the incoming *Canada.*

IRENE - *Masts Were Cut away*

The *Boston Post Marine Journal* divulged in a stereotypic entry that "The vessel . . . reported ashore at Fawn Bar, Boston Harbor, is the ship *Irene* of New York, Captain Williams, which sailed from Liverpool December 1, for Boston, with a general cargo of merchandise. She struck on Winthrop Bar at 8 o'clock on Sunday morning. Her masts were cut away, and the same evening she went ashore on Point Shirley Beach between the Copper Works and the Head. The crew were all saved. One man had his leg fractured by the falling masts. The *Irene* was built at Essex, Ct., in 1851."

Another entry was about the craft that was wrecked on January 13, 1856: "The *Irene* had 10 feet of water in her hold at high water today, and the tide ebbs and flows in her. The underwriters have their agents near the wreck and every exertion will be made to save the property. The ship may be got off." The vessel carried salt, earthenware, copper sheathing, iron bars, and an assortment of other products.

CAROLINE - *The Herrings Washed Out*

"Br. Sch. *Caroline*, from Fortune Bay, NF, for Boston, with a cargo of herrings in bulk, consigned to Thomas J. Jones, went ashore this morning in the snowstorm on Deer Island." The *Boston Daily Advertiser* further reported: "The crew landed in the morning with exception of the captain. He remained on board until there was no chance of saving his vessel, when he was taken off by Messrs. Jas. M. Dolliver and P. H. Chandler, who succeeded in rescuing him in a canoe after two unsuccessful attempts had been made by a lifeboat from Deer Island. At last account the sch. was on her beam ends at the SE end of the Island. Her bottom is badly stove and the herrings washed out."

During the February 3, 1859, incident, the force of the seas rolling over the bar kept the lifeboat from making headway. As a result the pilot boat *Friend* launched the canoe and plucked the captain off as he was about to heave himself overboard, hoping to be washed ashore.

MINNA - *A Cargo of Ancient Cannon*

An exceptional wreck was that of the schooner *Minna* between Deer Island and Winthrop Head on January 14, 1874. An iron craft of sixty-three tons, registered out of Yarmouth, Nova Scotia, she was flung ashore in a fierce storm with her cargo of ancient iron cannon. The heavily laden *Minna* was abandoned in seven feet of water and became embedded up to her deck in sand. The sails and rigging tore away, and the hull filled. Under Captain Shaw, she was bound from Port-au-Prince to Boston. Cannon valued at $3,000, and destined to ornament Boston parks, had been purchased from Haitian government officials by a Mr. James Power, a Bostonian.

Mr. Power had to buy his own cannon again for $25 at a salvage auction on the beach. A few days later the *Minna* was pumped out and towed to Boston by the tugs *Camilla* and *Louis Osborne*. Historians have erroneously reported that the vessel sank in Broad Sound and that the cannon were never recovered.

JULIET - *Prisoners to the Rescue*

When the granite-laden schooner *Juliet* was wrecked between Deer Island Prison and Winthrop Head on January 9, 1886, three men were carried overboard by the furious waves that swept her fore and aft. The rest of the crew found temporary safety in the swaying rigging, but were lashed by biting wind and freezing spray. A lifeboat was efficiently manned by prisoners incarcerated at Deer Island. All volunteers, they were led by the prison's deputy superintendent.

The trip through the wild surf was extraordinarily perilous, but once clear she was taken in tow by a tug that was standing by, then released to windward of the wreck. A white ring of foaming sea surrounded the schooner, preventing a close approach. The sailors jumped overboard, reached the outstretched hands of the heroic inmates, and were drawn from death.

GOLDSMITH MAID - *Stern Sank in the Narrows*

On the night of November 6, 1888, the steamer *Glaucus*, heading out of the harbor for New York, ran down the Gloucester fishing schooner *Goldsmith Maid*. Two of the crew, Howard Munroe and Peter Lundrey, both of Nova Scotia, were trapped in the forecastle and drowned. The stern sank in the Narrows, and the forward part was towed to Gallop's Island and beached. The vessel, owned by W. H. Gordon, was under Captain Hines. She was built in Bath, Maine, in 1871, totaled 48.68 tons, and was insured under the Gloucester Mutual Fishing Insurance Company for $24,000, including equipment.

Captain Hines later disclosed, "While coming into the Narrows last night, about 6:45 o'clock, with a southwest wind, we saw a steamer with lights showing, bearing down on us. We immediately luffed, thinking the steamer would keep off, but instead she kept on the same course, and before we could do anything further she crashed into us, striking the vessel on the starboard side, forward of the fore rigging, and cutting her in two."

CLARA S. CAMERON - *Wrecking Master at Scene*

Boston Post Marine Notes reported: "Fishing schooner *Clara S. Cameron* of Dennis, from Georges [Bank], with about 22,000 pounds of fish is ashore at Fort Warren. She went ashore at 10 o'clock Thursday night (November

5, 1891) and is full of water. Two tugs made an unsuccessful attempt to pull her off yesterday, and it is quite probable she will go to pieces."

A follow-up article a few days later stated: "A wrecking master with the tug *Elsie* and lighter *Elm* have gone down the harbor to remove the ballast from the fishing schooner *Clara S. Cameron* before reported ashore at Fort Warren. After the ballast is taken out casks will be placed aboard and around the schooner and an attempt will be made to float her." Four tugs finally pulled her off, but many, including the press, assumed that the Georges Island wreck was a total loss.

WILLIAM S. SLATER - *Hit Devil's Back Ledge*

The oceangoing tugboat *William S. Slater,* of the Boston Towboat Company, steamed onto treacherous Devil's Back on August 26, 1892. Darkness had begun to set in, the weather thickened, and the captain became disoriented in his navigational calculations. All aboard safely abandoned the mortally damaged vessel. A few hours later, the tug slid off the ledge into deeper water, canceling all hope of saving her. Such a valuable craft may ultimately have been salvaged.

The *William S. Slater* is described as having an iron hull, two masts, 60 foot length, and 63 tons net register. She was built in Philadelphia in 1881, insured for $25,000, and carried a crew of nine.

MARY ELIZA - *Vestiges Strewn along Shore*

The coasting schooner *Mary Eliza* was driven on Cottage Hill Bar, off Point Shirley, Winthrop, on February 8, 1895, floating off with a gaping hole in her hull. Hauling 107 tons of baled hay, the vessel had been stalled by a heavy snow squall. Captain Morrissey lowered both anchors, but the lines parted and she pitched ashore near Shirley Gut, a total loss. Her remains were spread all along the shore. The crew barely escaped with their lives and the clothes they wore. A collection was taken up for the mariners, furnishing them with the basic necessities and transportation to Boston.

The *Mary Eliza* was fifteen years old and uninsured, her owners preferring to take the risk themselves rather than pay the rate demanded by the underwriters. The vessel was valued at $2,000 and the cargo at $1,000. The deeper water near Shirley Gut has great potential for adventurers seeking vanished craft.

CADET - *Formerly Stationed at West Point*

The Lynn and Nahant Steamship Company passenger boat *Cadet,* which served the 1st Heavy Artillery Regiment, Fort Warren, went to pieces at

Shirley Gut on April 28, 1898. The *Cadet* registered 65 tons, was 88 feet long, and had been stationed at West Point Military Academy on the Hudson River. The steamer was attempting to pass through the narrow Gut, but was blown onto the rocks at the channel mouth. The impact stove holes in the hull and severed the upper deck, which floated off through the Gut. The extremely high seas soon broke up the hull and nothing could be salvaged. The crew barely escaped drowning.

The police boat *Guardian* and two tugs attempted to render assistance, but they did not dare venture close to the wreck. The *Cadet* was carrying about 3,000 feet of lumber, fifteen barrels of bread, and other foodstuffs for the troops at Fort Warren.

FORTUNA - *Skipper's Wife among the Bravest*

January 24, 1908—In a storm described as the worst since the steamer *Portland* went to her hidden grave in 1898, a woman and seven men faced death in the harbor. The three-masted schooner *Fortuna,* under Captain Edward Leighton, was struck by the violent storm and swept into the breakers off the northeast side of Lovell's Island.

Mrs. Leighton, the skipper's wife, was described as "one of the bravest of the little band. When the seas were making a complete breach over the craft she encouraged the men. She did not fear; she believed the schooner that had weathered many a storm would come through all right." Those on the vessel escaped the ordeal unscathed, and they were picked up. The *Fortuna* was among the largest three-masters afloat. She was 152 feet long, 34.5 feet in the beam, with 14.5 depth of hold, and in ballast at the time.

DAVIS PALMER - *Diver Explores Wreck*

Captain William C. Sparrow, of the U.S. Life Saving Service at Stony Beach, reported that the foundered schooner *Davis Palmer,* a five-master, "lies across Broad Sound in about seven fathoms of water on a hard, rocky bottom. The position is about one mile northeast of Commissioner's Ledge. Capt. Sparrow is of the opinion that the vessel was lying at anchor and heading in the eye of the wind when she went down, and he also thinks that her bottom was pounded out. No bodies were discovered and Capt. Sparrow says that in all probability, when the bodies are found, they will be lashed to the rigging." The *Davis Palmer,* heavy with coal, was lost with all hands on December 26, 1909.

A later account advises that "diver Michael L. Frazer made several descents, exploring the wreck but finding no bodies. The decks were found to be littered with wreckage, and this seriously interfered with his work. He was unable to get into the forecastle, while some of the other parts of the hull were so clogged with broken fittings as to render a minute examination impossible."

M. H. READ - *On The Teeth of the Ledge*

The *Boston Post* provided readers with a graphic account of this October 1, 1911, calamity.

> *The schooner* M. H. Read *hard and fast on the rocks off Ram's Head Light, Lovell's Island, where she struck late Sunday night, was abandoned by her crew yesterday morning after a night of terror, and last night lay a helpless wreck, grinding to pieces on the teeth of the ledge, each wave breaking over the decks.*
>
> *Each heavy sea pitched the schooner forward on the rocks that bit deeper into the hull with every lurch. The lumber, lashed together on the deck, was all that saved her from going to pieces. Just before daybreak, worn out by the night's battle, numbed by the icy rain and thoroughly drenched by the seas, Captain Grant and his men sent a rocket into the sky.*
>
> *At dawn the lifeboat from the Stony Beach lifesaving station was sighted from the deck breasting the waves off shore. The lifesavers fought the breakers for two hours before they finally reached the schooner's side and took off the half-conscious men.*

ALBERTA - *Each Man for Himself*

Daniel Sullivan, a survivor from the capsizing of the sloop *Alberta* in Black Rock Channel off Lovell's Island, told the press about eight passengers lost in the July 14, 1913, tragedy. "It was a case of each man for himself, for it came to pass that the waves were sweeping over the *Alberta,* and just when you thought that you had a firm grip, you were swept into the water again. Skipper Ayres was at the wheel when the blow hit us. He did not have a chance to luff her into the wind before the wind struck us on the starboard quarter and blew the boat over as if she were a chip. At the time I think that there were two or three in the cabin. Following the upset I did not see them again."

Another account indicates that the disaster took place approximately where lines would intersect north from Ram's Head Bar and west of Deer Island Light.

ACTOR - *Collision with Quartermaster Boat*

The U.S. Army quartermaster boat *General Batchelder* and the two-masted fishing schooner *Actor* collided between Fort Strong and Fort Standish in dense fog on September 26, 1924. The *Actor,* carrying 20,000 pounds of cod, was struck resoundingly on the starboard side; the larger military boat kept her from going down, however, by keeping her bow lodged in the schooner's hull. Most of the crew were helped onto the *General Batchelder.*

As the fishing craft sank, two men became tangled in the ropes and went under with her. Luckily, both worked themselves free and popped to the surface. Private Harold Dawes and Sergeant Leonard Potter of Company L, 11th Infantry, jumped over the side and helped the fishermen stay afloat. Aboard the *General Batchelder* were thirty to forty children on the way to public school in Hull. The many young dependents of military personnel on board could well have been lost.

MARY E. O'HARA - *Seamen Dropped into Eternal Darkness*

The *Mary E. O'Hara,* a fishing schooner, was entering the outer harbor in gusty winds during the early morning darkness of January 21, 1941. Without warning, she careened off an anchored barge on which no lights were visible. The impact punched a hole in her hull and she rapidly filled. The men, shaken by the collision, managed to find temporary safety in the rigging as the craft rapidly sank one-half mile east of Finn's Ledge buoy.

The vessel slid under in thirty-five to forty-five feet, the rigging thrusting above the choppy surface. Freezing weather made some of the crew lose their grip. As frozen fingers lost strength, one by one, several seamen dropped into eternal darkness. A lookout on a passing trawler spotted the masts through the dim light, and it picked up five survivors in the last agonies of clinging to the precarious perch.

LYNN - *Trapped Like Sardines in a Can*

A *Boston Globe* article on November 29, 1951, told of a disaster: "The 10,000 ton tanker *Ventura* smashed into the stern of the 170-ton trawler *Lynn* in outer Boston Harbor last night and sank her. Fifteen Greater Boston fishermen perished. Only two of the 17 were rescued. Two others were plucked from the icy water but never regained consciousness. Within the steel-jacketed hull 13 more were trapped below deck like sardines in a can when the trawler sank in a matter of seconds."

"I couldn't even give a warning," said the trawler's helmsman. "The ship flopped over like a fish on the starboard side. Then a gush of water raged into the wheelhouse, sweeping him and the skipper back into the latter's cabin. But they got out through an open window, only to be sucked 20 feet down into the surging sea."

The *Lynn* had been followed by another trawler, the *Bollard*. Robert Thorwaldson, of Hough's Neck, and a *Bollard* crewman, had shipmates grasp his feet while he hung over the frigid sea and snatched four men from a watery tomb. The collision, like that of the *Mary E. O'Hara*, took place at the end of the North Channel off Finn's Ledge, about half a mile east of black-and-white Baker buoy, and halfway between Graves Light and Winthrop. The *Lynn* was raised ten months later, refitted, and renamed the *Gulf Stream*.

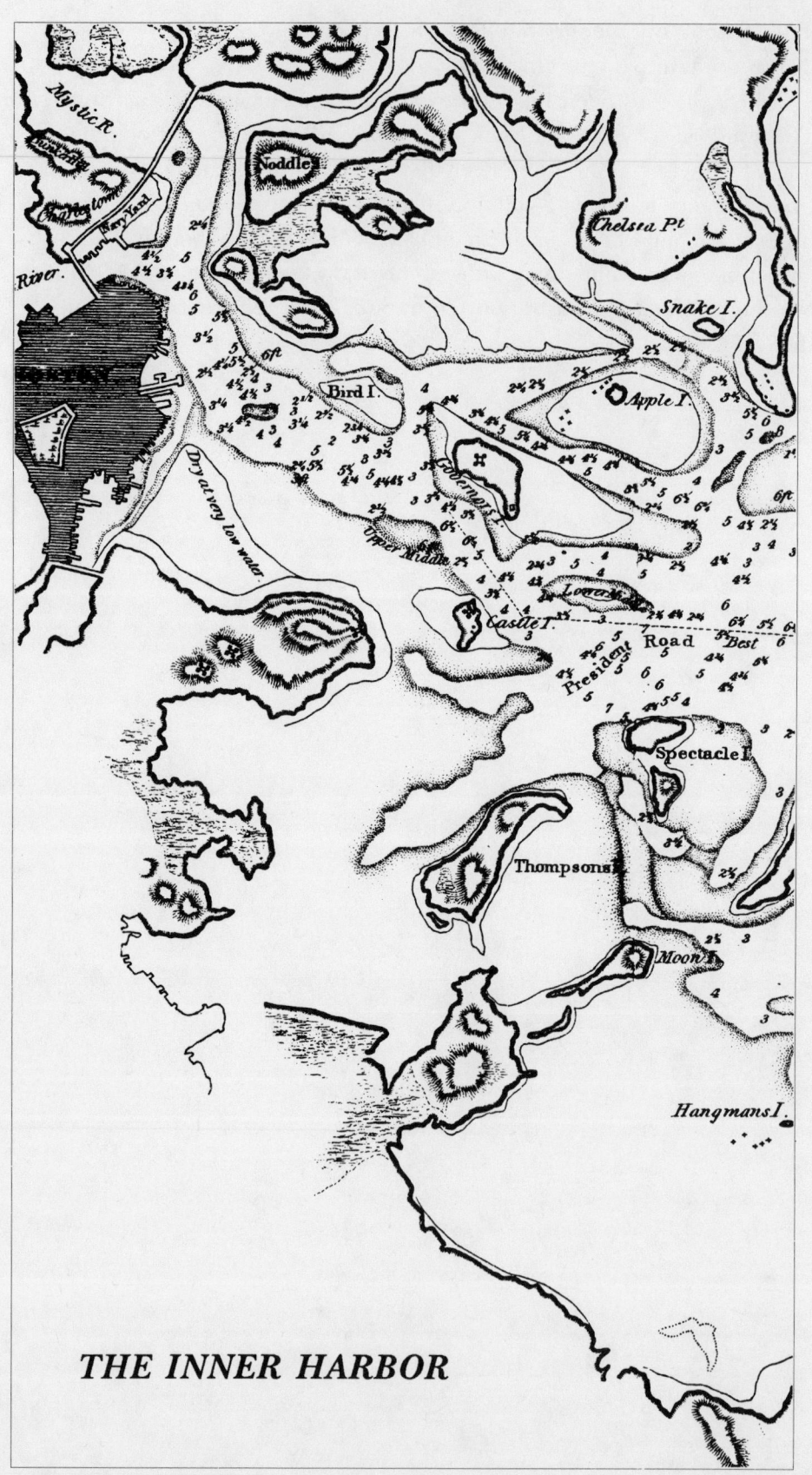

THE INNER HARBOR

The Inner Harbor

—⚓—

Boston and Inner-Islands Shipwrecks

The City of Boston overlooks an amphitheater of blue harbor with mosaic-like bits and pieces of islands. Lights of the metropolis sometimes create a nimbus above the waters, and in foreboding weather they may illuminate low clouds sailing past.

Nearby at the Charlestown Navy Yard (also known as the Boston Naval Yard), the freshening tide might barely sway the tall wooden ships such as the legendary *Constitution.* The forty-four-gun frigate, launched from Hart's Shipyard, Boston, in 1797, calls the Navy Yard her home port. Old Ironsides defeated the British frigates *Guerrière* and *Java* during War of 1812 naval engagements and captured the *Cyane* and *Levant,* both sloops-of-war. The figurehead of the docked frigate was lost from the bow on a stormy night in 1834, not by buffeting waves or chafing against another ship, but because the bust of Hercules was said to resemble too closely the politician Andrew Jackson.

The spectrum of famous vessels built at the Navy Yard ranges from the seventy-four-gun *Independence,* America's first ship-of-the-line. Launched in 1814, she engaged in action against the Barbary pirates. The steam sloop-of-war *Hartford* was sent down the ways in 1858, serving as Admiral David G. Farragut's flagship during duty against the Confederates at New Orleans and other southern ports. A double-turreted monitor, the *Monadnock,* launched in 1863 and assigned to Civil War blockade service became the first of her design to round Cape Horn. The *Mugford,* a destroyer launched in 1935, was once captained by Admiral Arleigh Burke and took part in many World War II battles in the Pacific. The *USS Gwin,* another destroyer, escorted the aircraft carrier *Hornet* on the first Tokyo bombing mission.

View of the ropewalk at the Charlestown Navy Yard

Yard of the Marine barracks, Charlestown Navy Yard

A hilarious waterfront spectacle took place at Mystic Wharf in Charlestown. During an unusually wild day in 1914, almost a hundred chattering monkeys and an uncooperative orangutan escaped from the docked British steamship *Montrose*. The animals were hanging by their tails from the cross-spars, as others scampered about the deck, chased by the Chinese crew. Embarrassed British ship's officers urged on the crew's efforts, and the captain was almost bowled over in the mélée. Hundreds of spectators gathered to witness the strange scene, applauding each comical capture.

The crescent-shaped mainland and inner archipelago have also experienced wrecks. When the Redcoats evacuated Boston in 1776, forty-five vessels were left behind sunken or dismasted. Tons of armaments and other military devices had been jettisoned, primarily along the waterfront. Following the evacuation, General George Washington assigned several teams of men to recover the more reachable spoils of war that had been thrown off Long Wharf and other nearby docks.

Recently, underwater explorers have expressed interest in recovering the tea chests that caused such a tempest during the Boston Tea Party. So much of Boston proper is now fill, however, that the chests could be buried under a waterfront skyscraper's foundation. If not, harbor silt may have preserved the artifacts in fairly good condition.

Closer to our times, a floating U.S. Life Saving Service station was maintained during the summer months just off Marine Pier in South Boston. In the most dangerous months during vicious gales, the vessels at anchor on the flats or trafficking the inner harbor are still at nature's mercy. Such Boston Police Department patrol and rescue boats as *Guardian* and *Protector* have performed admirably in emergencies.

During the "most spectacular fire in the history of the Boston Waterfront," the Boston Floating Hospital was enveloped in flames that marked her end on June 1, 1927. No lives were lost as the mercy ship burned to the waterline at a pier in North End Park.

Post card showing floating U.S. Life Saving Service Station (**Courtesy: Hull Lifesaving Museum**)

The islands that have more and significant wreck sites include Peddock's, Rainsford, Long, Spectacle, Thompson's, Castle, Governor's, Apple, and Nut.

Peddock's Island, with the longest shoreline on the western side of Hull Gut, has a tradition that an early 1600s plague ship came ashore in the northern cove. A virus is said to have spread among the Indian tribes, decimating them before Massachusetts settlers arrived. In 1614 or so, the island had Boston Harbor's first known shipwreck, which was related by Pecksuot, a local Sagamore. A Massachusetts Humane Society refuge hut once stood on the island.

Patriotic militia raided Peddock's during the War of Independence and removed several hundred livestock, ensuring lean times for British troops fortified in Boston.

In 1900 the U.S. Army designated the eastern end as Fort Andrews, and it soon bristled with twelve-inch mortars and three-inch and six-inch artillery. Antiaircraft guns were added during World War II.

A denuded drumlin roughly 200 yards long, connected to the southern shore, is called Prince's Head.

Some old charts called a bit of exposed shoal off Peddock's northwestern end Sunk Island.

Diminutive Rainsford Island, once known as Quarantine Island, sticks above the ocean surface near the entrance to the Western Way Channel. It is the only island on which a vessel, the *H. Davenport,* was cast ashore twice in separate gales.

A quarantine station stood on the island from 1737 to the mid-nineteenth century, recalled by touching epitaphs, etched into the ledges, telling of those who terminated life's voyages on this rocky strand. From a high hummock on the eastern end, you can see the entire island and surrounding harbor. Several hundred souls are interred there, most of them in unmarked graves. The elevation would be a beautiful setting in which to erect a cross or other memorial, both for those who were sent to the island to die, and for those whose identities have been erased by time or tide.

Between Spectacle and Rainsford lies Long Island, the harbor's largest. Governor John Winthrop, in a 1637 letter to his son, wrote: "A pinnace was cast away on Long Island by Nantascott." This is one of the earliest colonial references to a local shipwreck. A pinnace normally had two masts, was sharp fore and aft, and was employed in both trading and fishing.

As on other harbor islands, Continental soldiers and British marines skirmished here during the Revolutionary War. The island also served as burial ground for Civil War veterans who expired of disease on Rainsford Island.

Loading ballast at Long Island, Boston Harbor

Long Island Head had a fixed iron light around 1819. Visible for fifteen miles, the lighthouse was in a square enclosure that held the keeper's cottage and a fine fresh-water well. The present light tower stands on the northeast bluff and is solar powered.

An October 15, 1865, notation in the log of P. B. Small, keeper of Long Island Light, reveals that the schooner *Joseph Fish*, with 1,200 barrels of petroleum, was rammed while lying at anchor in Nantasket Roads, and "she immediately took fire by the overturning of the stove and was totally destroyed."

A June 13, 1897, wreck notation in an old mariner's scrapbook relates: "Captain Sorensen of the excursion steamer *Philadelphia*, who succeeded in pulling the wrecked fishing schooner *Jennie P. Phillips* from Harding's Ledge, where she stranded last Sunday morning, reports that he beached the vessel on the south side of Long Island, where an examination at low water revealed her starboard side is entirely gone and that the vessel is beyond repair."

The island heights later masked the formidable twelve-inch batteries of Fort Strong, honoring Major General George C. Strong, killed in the War Between the States. The parade ground reverberated with hundreds of marching troops during World War I. The 1st Battalion, 101st Infantry, pride of the Massachusetts Yankee Division, currently trains there.

The sizable keel and ribs of an unidentified wooden vessel are exposed at low water on Long Island's north shore. The barely recognizable vestiges of old wrecks can be found washed up on the beach.

On the southern side is Western Way Channel, formerly traveled by

Long Island Light, Boston Harbor

smaller coastal craft. President's Roads, once known to seafarers as King's Roads, separates Long Island from Deer Island at the northerly end.

Spectacle Island, as the name implies, originally was two islets connected by a short gravel isthmus that was covered at high tide. A few years after King Philip's War, we read, a ship was quarantined off Spectacle with small-

pox aboard. Boston residents went aboard to visit, though, and the terrible disease ultimately swept away many lives. The need for a harbor quarantine station was now obvious; one was established in 1717, and two decades later it was relocated to Rainsford Island.

Two range lights on the northern bluff long ago were destroyed by fire. The first was at latitude 42° 19' 40" and longitude 70° 59' 03", and the second was to the rear at 250 degrees and about 112 yards distant. The octagonal towers,

Spectacle Island Range Light

completed in 1897, were built of spruce, shingled and painted white. A snug wooden-frame keeper's house, combining barn and fuel-storage area, battery shed, and boathouse were nearby. Lining up the red range lights, a captain could safely guide a vessel on the final leg to Boston's waterfront.

The dark waters on the west side conceal rotting and rusting pieces from vessels that were run up into the shallows to waste away. For several years Mrs. Ann Sherwin made her home on the four-masted schooner *Snetind*, which later burned and was towed to the dumping grounds outside the harbor.

The island also received one of the larger wrecks, the 3,927-ton steamer *Ohio* of the Wilson Line, blown ashore with minimal damage in the 1898 Portland storm. During the gale the pilot boat *Columbia*, which had manned out her last pilot to the *Ohio*, was cast up on the beach at Scituate; all remaining hands were lost.

The U.S. submarine *L-50* rammed twenty feet of steel prow into the Nantasket steamer *Mayflower* on August 11, 1917, between Spectacle and Castle islands. Both vessels remained afloat.

Schooner Snetind *on Spectacle Island* (**Courtesy: Peabody Museum of Salem**)

The City of Boston used Spectacle Island for a dump, then neglected it for years, further polluting the harbor. During the 1930s some officials thought that planting flowers and shrubs on the island would offset adverse odors. Boston Harbor, they anticipated, would be a floral and historic gateway to the United States. In later years the island was plagued by subsurface fires at the dump.

Thompson's Island, which had the first Massachusetts trading post, antedated the Boston settlement. On the northwestern beach the tides wash through timbers from several wasted hulks. The island became home to the Boston Farm and Trade School, later Thompson's Academy, both having distinguished graduates.

Sadly, on April 29, 1842, *Polka,* a school sailboat, went under, taking with her twenty-three youngsters and two instructors.

America's great author Nathaniel Hawthorne made an enjoyable visit, during which he wrote a few lines about "vessels flitting past; great ships with intricacy of rigging and various sails; schooners, sloops, with their one or two broad sheets of canvas; going on different tacks, so that the spectator might think that there was a different wind for each vessel, or that they scudded across the sea spontaneously, whither their own wills led them."

Approach channels to Boston are under the granite gun casements at Fort Independence on Castle Island, anciently known as Castle William, for King William IV. This colonial Gibraltar, the oldest American military post, was founded by the pilgrim forefathers in 1634.

The fort's cannon have fired warning shots across the bows of ships thought to be on questionable missions. One errant gunner miscalculated his aim, and rather than dropping the round in front of the vessel, he killed a passenger resting in the rigging. The accident was judged to have been caused by an act of God: slow-burning powder and suddenly freshening wind in the vessel's sails.

Funds for keeping the fort in reasonable repair and readiness were often meager, worrying local military officials. During 1679, the entire garrison consisted of only a commander, a gunner, and four men to serve thirty cannon.

Mohawk Indians visiting the fort in 1709 were given a respectful military salute. Further, it confined Indians who had raised the war club, but in 1725 some succeeded in escaping, and fled back to the forest.

As they evacuated Boston Harbor in 1776, the Redcoats blew up the fort. In turn, twenty-one of the thirty-two-pound cannon from the British sixty-four-gun man-o'-war *Somerset,* which had been wrecked at Cape Cod in 1778, were Americanized in reconstructing the defenses. Gunners tested the Castle Island batteries by blasting away at the outer point on

The Boston Farm and Trade School, at Thompson's Island, Boston Harbor

Bird's eye view of Fort Independence, Boston Harbor

Thompson's Island. In ceremonies attended by President John Adams, the garrison was renamed Fort Independence.

Just below Castle Island on January 18, 1886, a rare triple collision involved the Norwegian fruit steamer *Vera,* the steam collier *Melrose,* and the four-masted schooner *Malcolm Baxter, Jr.* All vessels remained afloat.

The design wizardry of Donald McKay, father of the fast but highly specialized clipper ships, is celebrated on a prominent monument facing the channel.

Patrick J. Connolly, in his *Islands of Boston Harbor* (1936), comments: "From the birth of the colonies until 1882, every pulse of the colony's and nation's struggle in warfare, invasions and Indian uprisings, was centered on this Island. No page in the history of the world is more interesting, more romantic, more true of a people's struggle for peace and tranquility than that pertaining to Castle Island in Boston Harbor."

Directly across the channel from Castle Island is Governor's Island. Briefly called William's Island for a privateer captain, it has also been called Conant's Island and Winthrop's Island.

In a sudden storm on March 5, 1776, British troopships were blown aground on Governor's Island Flats. Although damage was minor, the winds foiled a planned landing at the rear of American soldiers besieging Boston.

Compilers of histories have asserted, but never clearly proved, that a heavy chain extended along the harbor bottom from Fort Winthrop, Governor's Island, to Castle Island. If the military need arose, a winch would raise the chain to halt any vessels. A winch of some type had been observed many years back, but the system apparently was never completed. Much later, Governor's Island was leveled, not by gunfire but by bulldozers constructing Logan International Airport.

Vessels that were too decrepit to ply the sea lanes were sometimes left to waste away on Governor's Island Flats. On a clear day from the air you can see in outline a large wooden wreck imprinted on the muddy bottom.

The Apple Island Flats were also frequented by wreckers, extracting valuable iron and copper salvage from incinerated craft. Many ships had an inglorious end in a funeral pyre on a mud flat.

Oliver Wendell Holmes named the heartless among these wreckers "Harpies of the land." The *Canton Packet,* a ship of some notoriety from a harbor explosion, was one of the first burned for scrap at Apple Island. Rustic summer dwellings here were constructed almost entirely of steamer stateroom panels and doors.

Incidentally, the island was named, not for large apple trees that some sailors mistakenly believed spread their boughs there, but because on early charts the shoreline was shaped like an apple. A ninety-five-foot-high elm (not an apple tree) was in fact a useful guide to mariners. The ancient landmark, mentioned in an Oliver Wendell Holmes poem, was hacked down by vandals in 1938.

Nut Island, just off Hough's Neck, Quincy, was one of the last wrecking places and a test site for experimenting with large cannon. Among the guns echoing across the harbor were those installed on the *Monitor,* which blazed away against the *Merrimac* in their heralded Civil War encounter. A mammoth cannonball is rumored to have missed its target on Prince's Head, Peddock's Island, skipping dangerously across the water toward Hull. An angry outburst from the town's citizens put an end to the tests.

A local reporter wrote with rather poetic emphasis about Nut Island's victimized ships: "There is something pathetic and sorrowful about these old remains as they lie smoldering and smoking, the sun glinting and gleaming on their copper covered hulls, the water which they so dearly loved greedily and impatiently lapping them, as if desiring to once again feel them gliding majestically across its bosom, while the rough wreckers are cutting and hacking their very vitals."

The USS *Wyoming,* a warship in Commodore Perry's squadron, which opened Japan for trade in 1854, fell under the torch and wrecking bar in 1893. Sidewheel steamers such as the beautiful *Katahdin,* which was stranded locally and saved, also were rendered into charred timbers. In 1891 the USS *Brooklyn,* at one time Admiral Farragut's flagship, was sent up in flames. Nearby a few homesteads were assembled from cabins torn from various steamers, and staterooms and first-class berths were recycled into unique sleeping quarters.

Directly off the northern end of the island is Wreck Rock, on which the ribs of a wooden vessel could be seen at low tide.

In relatively recent years the harbor's ship boneyard was Chelsea Creek, on the East Boston side. Vessels, some once renowned but no longer seaworthy and destined for the scrap pile, were towed to these mud flats.

One of those condemned was the *Yankton,* opulently built in Scotland in 1893 as the yacht for King Edward VII. Christened *Penelope,* she was later purchased by famed actress Sarah Bernhardt and renamed *Cleopatra.* A Massachusetts entrepreneur owned her in the mid-1800s, and shortly thereafter she was sold to the U.S. Navy for service in the Spanish-American War. Commissioned as *Yankton,* she was converted to a fast gunboat. After hostilities ceased, she took part in a trip around the world with the American fleet. During 1918 the craft was redesigned as a patrol boat, and while on World War I convoy duty in the Mediterranean was credited with sinking at least one enemy submarine. Decommissioned in

Steamer Yankton *blown ashore on Georges Island* (**Courtesy: Peabody Museum of Salem**)

1920, she came again into private ownership. Apparently the new owners' interests went beyond legitimate business, for in 1923 *Yankton* was
seized as a rumrunner.

In her later years the craft had a scheduled steamer route between St.
John's, Newfoundland, and Boston, but in 1925 she ran aground on Nix's
Mate. Once fit for a king, the vessel was no longer fit for any service and
was broken up for her scrap metal. A more honorable end would have
been burial at sea.

Before leaving the harbor shoreline we look into *Proceedings of the
Bostonian Society* about three Hub gentlemen famed in the early days of
American marine telegraphy: Jonathan Grout, Jr., who constructed the
first visual telegraph in the country; Samuel Topliff, who had a system for
collecting intelligence that was claimed to be almost on a par with the illustrious Lloyd's of London; and John R. Parker, who for many years operated the most proficient harbor telegraph in America and had a system of
visual signal code flags used on more than two thousand vessels.

In 1801, Grout sent shipping news from Woods Hole to Boston
through stations at Great Hill, Weymouth, and Dorchester Heights. The
last dispatch was communicated in 1807.

In 1810, Samuel Gilbert opened a commercial news chamber in the
Exchange Coffee House, Boston. Topliff, who took over the business in

1814, put it among the world's most renowned newsrooms. The operation was later moved to the Merchant's Exchange and Chamber of Commerce. These became favorite haunts for Boston merchants awaiting their long-absent captains and news from around the globe.

In 1820, Topliff extended the Boston Harbor telegraph from Fort Independence to Long Island Head. Instead of the usual semaphore or light with shutters, he used a mast with an arm and three black balls, hoisting private signal flags on a topmast.

Parker initiated his own enterprise during 1822, renting the dome in a Central Wharf building and setting up a semaphore station on Long Island Head. It was moved to Boston Lighthouse Island, then in 1825 to Point Allerton, supervised by Joseph Pope of Hull. The station was transferred to a new site during 1827, and named Telegraph Hill. Parker's relay stations were on Rainsford Island, and then Georges Island. An office in the Old State House was the base station.

American vessels had been assigned specific numbers so that between 1828 and 1844, when Parker sold the business, he had the longest shipping list in the nation.

Enhanced mid-19th-century view of the city of Boston, Massachusetts

The harbor lifesavers and wreckers alike watched the signal station for early warnings of disaster. As illustrated in the *Signal Book for Boston Harbor* (1848), combinations of flags identified individual vessels, and specific wreck signals were shown as well: No. 143 signaled "vessel ashore on Toddy Rocks," and No. 421 meant "vessel has gone to pieces."

In 1853 the magnetic telegraph was installed at Hull, and wreck notification could be quickly sent out over the telegraph.

UNIDENTIFIED - *Indians Burn Trading Vessel*

An old-time writer records that "The Indians thought the first ship was a walking island, and the masts were trees, the sails, white clouds; the discharge of ordnance, thunder and lightning, which did much trouble them." Obviously they had early contact with Frenchmen, for when English explorer Captain John Smith entered the outer harbor in 1614, he found that the French had been trading for weeks but had left nothing.

The earliest known incident leading to a wreck took place about 1614, when local Indians captured a French trading vessel off Peddock's Island. Her crewmen were slain, perhaps in retaliation for some injustice, and the craft was destroyed. Pecksuot, a prominent warrior, confided during an eyewitness account to an English chronicler: "Thus we killed them all. But Monseigneur Finch, master of their ship, being wounded, leaped into the hold. We bid him come up, but he would not. Then we cut their cable and the ship went ashore and lay upon her side and slept there. Finch came up and we killed him. Then our sachem divided their goods and fired their ship, and it made a very great fire."

GREAT HOPE - *1600s Ship Blown Ashore*

During the gale of August 15, 1635, the 400-ton ship *Great Hope* from Ipswich, England, with cargo, if any, unknown, was blown aground at a location identified as Hoffe's Point. As the wind shifted to the northwest the vessel was forced off, but she beached again near Charlestown. The change in wind was accompanied by a rare phenomenon—the tide coming in twice within twelve hours. The final disposition of the *Great Hope* was not described.

Thomas Morton, who observed the tremendous storm, wrote: "It blew down sundry houses, and uncovered divers [various] others, divers vessels were lost at sea, and many more were in extreme danger. It caused the sea to swell in some places to the southeast of Plymouth, so that it rose to twenty feet right up and down, and made of the Indians to climb into trees for their safety."

WARWICK - *A Colonial-Period Wreck*

One of the earliest wrecks identified by name was the bark *Warwick* of ten guns. Sailing the coast between the American colonies on errands of government and commerce, the craft temporarily led a charmed existence but barely escaped the Point Allerton rocks in 1631. She is claimed to have come to an end near the mouth of Neponset River in 1636. The constable of Dorchester was ordered to inventory and appraise the vessel. Warwick Cove and Barque Warwick Street appear on older maps, substantiating that such an incident took place.

Such a vessel's remains would be a major archeological discovery, especially if preserved from oxidation by silt, but probably the *Warwick* was salvaged, or removed by channel dredging.

MARY ROSE - *Gold Fired from Cannon*

Governor Winthrop tells about the *Mary Rose* from Bristol, England, ten guns, about 200 tons, which was anchored off Charlestown on July 27, 1640. The captain and crew were encouraged by local clergy to attend church; they refused, however, claiming their own service aboard was as good as that ashore. Within two hours, twenty-one kegs of gunpowder exploded, killing all on board except one man, who was saved by being borne up and set down in the scuttle (hatch). He regained consciousness next morning but could provide no clue to the origin of the blast. A gold coin was found sticking in a fragment of wood, for the ship carried about 300 English pounds, plus fifteen tons of lead and armament.

Winthrop's journal reveals that the owners were under court decree to free the harbor, "which was much damnified by her." About two years later, Edward Bendall of Boston undertook to remove the hulk. Bendall fashioned a crude wooden diving bell, in which he was able to remain underwater nearly half an hour. He fastened ropes to the ordnance and placed other articles in nets, which were drawn to the surface by tenders.

About thirty pounds in specie were rumored to be hidden in one of the *Mary Rose*'s cannon. The guns were recovered, searched, and a hefty wad of rope yarn was discovered in one of them. Assuming it was heavy because it was wet, gunners threw the material on the deck to dry. Several days later, as the men tested a cannon, they inserted the wad with a powder charge and shot it toward the channel. A portion broke off and fell short, and the rest landed in midchannel. On the next low tide, gold and silver coins were discovered where no treasure had been found before. The coins apparently had been secreted inside the yarn and spewed over the water when the cannon was fired.

DIANA - *Patriots Burn British Warship*

In his diary, loyalist Ezekiel Price tells about the battle of Chelsea.

> *1775, Saturday, May 27 . . . At two P.M., saw a number of rebels at Noddle's Island destroying the hay; and made the signal for landing the marines, and sent the* Diana *schooner round to cut off their retreat. She went as far as there was water but the marines drove them off the island. The rebels kept up a constant fire on the* Diana *from Hog Island and the main, which she returned with great spirit. At seven, she got all boats ahead to tow her. The rebels kept up a constant fire on the boats; which at last became so warm, that they were ordered to cast off. Unfortunately for her, a breeze sprung up, which set her in upon the rebel's shore. Notwithstanding all these circumstances, she was defended with great spirit until the tide quitted her.*

The provincials captured four double four-pounders, twelve swivels, rigging, sails, and other property from the British schooner. Bundles of hay were expeditiously placed under her stern and she was then burned to keep her from falling back into enemy hands. The *Diana* was left a charred hulk, ashore on the Winnisimet ferry ways, now just west of Chelsea Bridge.

CANTON PACKET - *Explosion Blows Stern off Vessel*

The *Canton Packet* blew up on May 30, 1817. The vessel was an exceptionally fine ship of 350 tons, employed in the India trade, ready to sail with a $400,000 general cargo, including specie and several casks of gunpowder. The ship was watched over by a disgruntled steward while the crew, on their last day in port, were enjoying festivities in Boston. During a moment of apparent madness, the steward allegedly discharged a pistol into the powder, blowing himself to smithereens and the stern off the vessel.

Some seamen on the nearby United States warship *Independence* cut the cable and ran the remainder of the wreck ashore on the flats just north of Long Wharf. The bizarre incident so stirred Boston that a ballad was even written about the infamous *Canton Packet*.

H. DAVENPORT - *Wrecked Twice on Hospital Island*

During extraordinary Atlantic Coast gales in December 1839, official reports stated that more than 90 vessels were lost and almost 200 driven ashore, dismasted, or otherwise damaged. On December 15, the British schooner *H. Davenport,* apparently in ballast, was thrown on Hospital Island, now known as Rainsford Island. At the same time the *Susanna,* another British craft, was cast up on the Quincy shore with little damage.

A second storm, less severe than the first, began on December 22. The *H. Davenport,* after much labor, had been refloated between storms, but the later gale again drove her onto the island, even more disabled. She had the rare but dubious distinction of being wrecked twice at the same place during different tempests.

NORMAN - *Hard-hat Divers Examine Steamer*

The steamer *Norman,* arriving in the harbor from Philadelphia on March 10, 1868, when about three miles from the Boston wharves, struck a ledge just off the Lower Middle shoal. She stove in her bottom and the rocks held her firmly. At high water the steamship's bow was visible, but the stern was well below the surface. The disaster was blamed on a buoy that guides vessels approaching the ledge; the buoy had been hidden because the top was broken off. The *Norman* had a valuable load of cotton, wool, drugs, iron, and steel.

Hard-hat divers inspected the steamer and observed significant damage to her hull. Once the cargo was removed, temporary repairs were made, the vessel was pumped out and refloated by casks around the hull. The *Norman* was saved to make several safe trips past the shoal that nearly caused her demise.

AVELON - *Crewmen and Deck Load Washed Over*

On November 26, 1888, the schooner *Avelon* from St. John, New Brunswick, with 940,000 laths, went ashore on Spectacle Island. Captain Mulberry was interviewed:

> He left St. John, Nov. 22, and had good weather as far as Mt. Desert, Me., when the wind headed to the northeast, but continued light until 8 A.M. Sunday, at which time the schooner reached the vicinity of Cape Cod. The wind then increased to a gale, with blinding snow and extremely high seas, which continually swept over the vessel, washing away the deckload of laths, and also two of the schooner's crew.
>
> The weather being too thick to proceed, he concluded to head for Boston. At about 2 P.M. on Sunday he discovered the breakers off Halfway Rock and let go the anchor. The chain parted, and the schooner again started for Boston. One of the crew was soon afterward struck by the mainboom, knocked overboard and lost. About 5 P.M. on Sunday he anchored off Spectacle Island and subsequently parted the remaining chain. The vessel was forced ashore and classified a total wreck.

VENETIAN - *When Sailors Became Cowboys*

A London-bound British steamship of the Furness Line, the *Venetian*, was heavily damaged when she stranded on the east side of Governor's Island Flats on March 2, 1895. The 423-foot vessel had a deck load of 643 head of cattle and 838 sheep. Twenty-three cattle were scalded to death when a steam line ruptured, and several others had to be put out of their misery. The four-masted steamship, which also carried wheat, quarters of fresh beef, flour, bacon, lard, cheese, and hay, struck Slate Ledge in a thick snow squall that blotted out navigational reference points.

The rocks stove a large hole in her steel plates, and had not the live-stock been on deck, all would certainly have perished. The herd was trans-ported ashore by lighters in a bizarre turn of occupation, as sailors became cowboys. It was not an easy task to force the distraught animals into a chute and onto the lighters. The *Venetian* cracked in half a short time later and was salvaged as scrap.

JOHN F. NICKERSON - *Marvelous Escape from Death*

"A few feet of mast and rigging that still protrude over the surface of the water is all that can now be seen of the trim fishing schooner *John F. Nickerson*. She was bravely beating up the harbor channel early last evening when suddenly there was a dull crash and the vessel went to the bottom, her crew having a most marvelous escape from death." Other news stories

Wrecked steamer Venetian *showing enterprising advertising* (**Courtesy: Peabody Museum of Salem**)

reveal that on the evening of October 25, 1895, after being struck by an unlit mud scow towed by a tug, the heavily laden schooner gave a pitch forward and plunged downward at the channel edge just off Fort Independence.

The news further related: "A second more and it would have been too late, for the men did not have time to lift the boats over the side, but just tumbled into them pell-mell, while the water rushing over the decks swept them free." The captain barely won his wild race with the sea as he took to the masthead with a rented sextant under his arm. The schooner carried a Cape Sable catch of several thousand pounds of halibut.

VIRGINIA - *Sea Began to Pour over Her*

So violent was the November 27, 1898, storm that even vessels in protected anchorages were dashed ashore. The coasting schooner *Virginia* of Mt. Desert, Maine, was off Fort Independence, Castle Island, in good holding ground when the blow began. The schooner, carrying wax, dragged on the northern portion of Thompson's Island, as did three others of her kind. She was a total wreck.

The young son of Captain Stanley said in an interview: "As soon as she took bottom she swung around broadside on the shore, and the sea began to pour over her. We took to the rigging and stayed there until the masts fell. That was some time after daylight, I should think. When the masts fell my father and Freeman were lost." Determined efforts were made to launch a rescue boat from the island, but it filled almost immediately in the crushing surf. The other schooners were in less precarious positions and were hauled off.

RESOLUTE - *Tug Settled Immediately*

A collision sank the United States government tug *Resolute* and killed her engineer on January 3, 1900, between Governor's Island and Castle Island. A report explains:

> *The* Resolute *was the Fort Warren boat and was making its regular evening trip down to the fort from Boston. Captain Loring took the customary route and had proceeded as far as buoy 9.*
>
> *He passed the steamer* Putnam, *which was inward bound from Lynn on the starboard side and was heading over to the side of the channel nearest Governor's Island, when he met the* Swatara *which was out in the harbor adjusting compasses preparatory to taking a tow of three empty barges to Philadelphia. The steel bow of the* Swatara *penetrated the wooden side of the* Resolute, *which began to settle immediately.*

CITY OF BOSTON - *Men Fought with Women*

"With the water pouring over her deck and through a hole in the bow and her passengers yelling and whistle blowing for help, the Chelsea ferryboat *City of Boston,* last night was just able to save herself from sinking by running her nose into East Boston flats. The panic on board was something fearful. The 28 passengers refused to be quieted by the boat's officers and lined the upper deck arrayed in life preservers, where the men fought the women to be first rescued." So ran a Boston news account.

On March 13, 1904, the old ferry had struck a waterlogged mud scow, and had to paddle for life to reach shallow water. When a lifesaving dory arrived, some men fought so violently to be taken off that the dory had to wait until calm prevailed. On the other hand, a drunk was found sleeping below deck amid the swirling waters, and until placed under arrest he stubbornly refused to be saved.

CITY OF BIRMINGHAM - *Struck Submerged Wreck*

The steamer *City of Birmingham* sank off Castle Island during the night of November 4, 1907, after striking a submerged wreck. She carried a heavy load of miscellaneous freight and was bound for Savannah, Georgia. The skipper was able to run her onto the mud flats at the channel edge. The crew abandoned ship in their own boats. No passengers were on board, and no lives were lost. At 3,066 tons, she settled quickly. Her upper deck and funnel were exposed at low tide.

A Gloucester, Massachusetts, fishing schooner discharging at commercial wharf, Boston

Divers examined the hull and found that several of her forward plates had been torn off, but the hole could be patched, the hull pumped out, and the steamer raised. The vessel was salvaged and towed to East Boston for extensive repairs.

R. L. TAY - *Schooner's Bow Ripped off*

Without warning the Nantasket steamer *Rose Standish* and lumber schooner *R. L. Tay* collided off Long Island about 7:30 P.M. on September 9, 1914. Close to a hundred passengers were badly frightened. The starboard paddlebox was damaged and the steering gear was out of commission. Captain Walker Rathburn immediately sent out a distress signal, though the steamer was not in deep trouble, but the schooner's bow was ripped off in the mishap.

The tug *George A. Hibbard*, which happened to be docked at Long Island, went to help the *R. L. Tay* and towed her to the island, where she was beached. The captain and crew were removed by the City Point lifesaving crew. United States steamboat inspectors were ordered to make an inquiry into the incident.

MARGUERITE - *Sank in Less Than Two Minutes*

At 3:30 on the morning of September 9, 1916, the *Marguerite* settled on the harbor bottom less than two minutes after the steam-lighter *Eureka* slammed into the sand-carrying schooner. Immediately after the collision, Captain Geyer and his four crewmen dashed for a dory towed astern of the *Marguerite*. They had barely severed the tow rope when the craft lurched forward and sank. They lost all personal items, including the captain's gold watch.

If the five men had all not been on deck at the time, some might have accompanied the schooner in her plunge. The *Eureka* picked them up from the dory and transported them to Boston. The two mast tops of the vessel were visible above the water at the channel's southern side, just below the South Boston State Pier. The *Marguerite*, a former fisherman constructed at Essex in 1883, was owned by Boston Sand & Gravel Company. She was listed at 88 feet long, 23.5 foot beam, 8.4 depth of hold, gross tonnage 109, and 81 net tons.

MAYFLOWER - *Submarine Ripped into Steamer*

On the fog-blanketed afternoon of August 11, 1917, like a deadly specter, U.S. Submarine *No. 50* silently cut through the waters off Spectacle Island.

The Fishing schooner Marguerite *sunk off South Boston.* (**Courtesy: Peabody Museum of Salem**)

Suddenly, as if out of nowhere, almost awash, she ripped twenty feet into the side of the Nantasket steamer *Mayflower,* which carried 700 passengers. With the fearful tearing and grating collision, terror swept the steamer's decks as many rushed for life preservers. Several women fainted in fright and had to be revived by fellow passengers. A few men panicked and grabbed life preservers dropped by alarmed women. Military personnel and crew members calmed the crowd.

Luckily, the almost-empty steamer *Rose Standish* of the same line loomed out of the mist and made fast to the side of the stricken *Mayflower.* Reassured men stood aside to allow women and children to abandon ship. In the boiler room, the *Mayflower* stokers resolutely remained at their posts, extinguishing the coal fires to prevent explosions should the sea pour in. The *Mayflower,* with the submarine still plugging the hole, was towed to safety. That evening the city was full of rumors that a German U-boat had attacked shipping in Boston Harbor.

EDWARD PEIRCE - *Engine Room Crew Waist Deep in Water*

The crippled collier *Edward Peirce* managed to reach the mud flats off South Boston in the "nick of time" before sinking. While being assisted by a tow-boat, the vessel collided with the outward-bound freighter *Mundelta* off Deer Island, on September 24, 1924. The collier, under command of

Captain Harold T. Ricker, carried 6,000 tons of coal and thus would have gone down rather quickly with the severe damage she sustained. Fortunately the tug *N. P. Doane* responded to the collier's whistles of desperation and managed to help push her safely through the harbor channels onto the flats. At the same moment that the *Edward Peirce* touched bottom the engine room boiler fires were extinguished by sea water flooding the compartments. The gutsy engine room crew were up to their waists in water. Special praise was reserved for Second Assistant Engineer Bragg, who continued working vital controls until water reached his armpits. At this point the mariners were forced to abandon their positions and leave the collier.

The *Edward Peirce* was owned by the Mystic Steamship Company, registered 4,388 tons, had a length of 354 feet, and was built in Newport News, Virginia, in 1914.

As the vessel's stern partially blocked the ship channel, it became a potential navigational hazard. Divers from the Scott Wrecking Company expeditiously surveyed the hull, patched up a gaping hole on the starboard side, and refloated her. After dry-dock repairs she was soon back in service.

PILGRIM BELLE - *Teenagers in a Carnival Mood*

The steamer *Pilgrim Belle* was run ashore on the southwestern side of Spectacle Island on June 22, 1955. Bound for Nantasket, she struck a submerged object in fog that the captain of the rescue tug *Orion* called "thick as tar." Most of the 272 passengers were teenagers celebrating the end of the school year and summer's promise. Being in good spirits, the teenagers remained in a carnival mood throughout the operation. One youngster remarked to Boston Police boat crew members, "We were dancing to rock-and-roll stuff on the decks, and when we hit that rock we really rolled."

Losing steam, the *Pilgrim Belle's* skipper managed to swing the craft around the rocky eastern beach of Spectacle Island. Locating a favorable site, he pointed the bow toward shore and eased her on. All the passengers were high in praise for the captain, because he acted quickly and wisely to avoid sinking.

The old Nantasket steamers had their share of predicaments over the years, but relatively able commanders kept calamitous wrecks with loss of life from blighting the line's safety record.

Major Wrecks
in Chronological Sequence

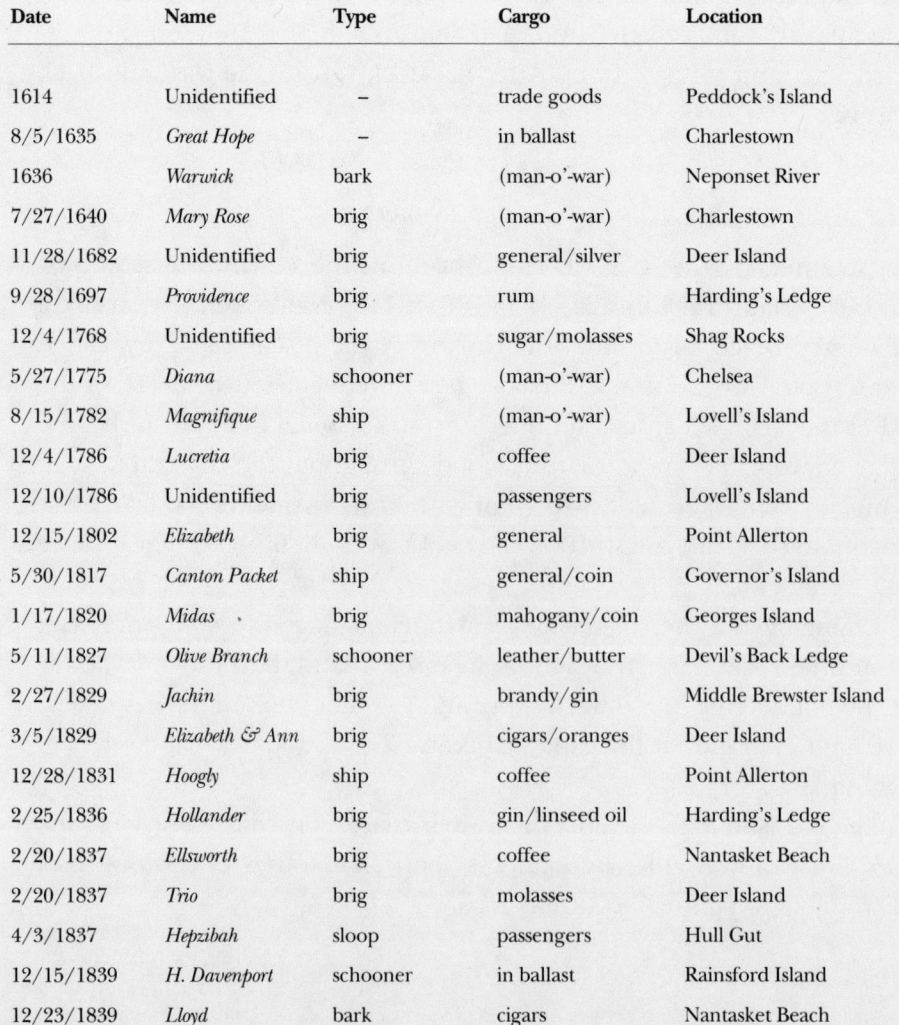

Date	Name	Type	Cargo	Location
1614	Unidentified	–	trade goods	Peddock's Island
8/5/1635	*Great Hope*	–	in ballast	Charlestown
1636	*Warwick*	bark	(man-o'-war)	Neponset River
7/27/1640	*Mary Rose*	brig	(man-o'-war)	Charlestown
11/28/1682	Unidentified	brig	general/silver	Deer Island
9/28/1697	*Providence*	brig	rum	Harding's Ledge
12/4/1768	Unidentified	brig	sugar/molasses	Shag Rocks
5/27/1775	*Diana*	schooner	(man-o'-war)	Chelsea
8/15/1782	*Magnifique*	ship	(man-o'-war)	Lovell's Island
12/4/1786	*Lucretia*	brig	coffee	Deer Island
12/10/1786	Unidentified	brig	passengers	Lovell's Island
12/15/1802	*Elizabeth*	brig	general	Point Allerton
5/30/1817	*Canton Packet*	ship	general/coin	Governor's Island
1/17/1820	*Midas*	brig	mahogany/coin	Georges Island
5/11/1827	*Olive Branch*	schooner	leather/butter	Devil's Back Ledge
2/27/1829	*Jachin*	brig	brandy/gin	Middle Brewster Island
3/5/1829	*Elizabeth & Ann*	brig	cigars/oranges	Deer Island
12/28/1831	*Hoogly*	ship	coffee	Point Allerton
2/25/1836	*Hollander*	brig	gin/linseed oil	Harding's Ledge
2/20/1837	*Ellsworth*	brig	coffee	Nantasket Beach
2/20/1837	*Trio*	brig	molasses	Deer Island
4/3/1837	*Hepzibah*	sloop	passengers	Hull Gut
12/15/1839	*H. Davenport*	schooner	in ballast	Rainsford Island
12/23/1839	*Lloyd*	bark	cigars	Nantasket Beach

Date	Name	Type	Cargo	Location
4/30/1841	*Emeline*	schooner	lumber	Point Allerton
6/19/1841	*Diana*	ship	passengers	Little Brewster Island
12/17/1841	*Mohawk*	ship	iron/anvils	Point Allerton
10/7/1844	*Tremont*	brig	molasses	Point Allerton
12/11/1844	*Massasoit*	ship	silks/indigo	Point Allerton
9/25/1847	*Surplus*	schooner	eggs/cordwood	Nantasket Beach
9/25/1847	*Nun*	schooner	lime	Gallup's Island
11/20/1848	*Oliver*	schooner	plaster	Point Allerton
4/8/1850	*L'Essai*	brig	brandy	Nantasket Beach
2/7/1851	*Carlos*	bark	cotton	Shag Rocks
1/4/1852	*Peerless*	schooner	flour	Nantasket Beach
11/25/1854	*Ocean*	steamer	passengers	Deer Island
1/13/1856	*Lewis*	schooner	general	Shag Rocks
1/13/1856	*Irene*	ship	general	Deer Island
3/2/1857	*Delaware*	ship	cotton	Stony Beach
3/2/1857	*Odessa*	brig	herring	Stony Beach
10/2/1857	*Harriet Ann*	schooner	coal	Harding's Ledge
1/17/1859	*Herald*	brig	sugar	Nantasket Beach
2/3/1859	*Caroline*	schooner	herring	Deer Island
3/10/1860	*Ewan Crerar*	brig	beer/arsenic	Outer Brewster Island
3/3/1861	*Enterprise*	schooner	flour	Shag Rocks
11/3/1861	*Maritana*	ship	wool/potash	Shag Rocks
1/19/1867	*Julia Anna*	schooner	flour	Little Brewster Island
3/10/1868	*Norman*	steamer	cotton/wool	Lower Middle Shoal
12/23/1870	*W. R. Genn*	schooner	coal	Nantasket Beach
12/26/1872	*Kadosh*	bark	hemp/sugar	Harding's Ledge
3/15/1873	*Helene*	schooner	hard pine	Point Allerton
1/13/1874	*Phantom*	sloop	(pilot boat)	Nantasket Beach
1/14/1874	*Minna*	schooner	cannon	Deer Island
3/31/1876	*Harriet Atwood*	schooner	oysters	Nantasket Beach
2/1/1882	*Chas. H. Lawrence*	schooner	coal	Outer Brewster Island
2/1/1882	*Fanny A. Pike*	schooner	coal	Shag Rocks
2/1/1882	*Grace Lothrop*	brig	oranges/cigars	Point Allerton
2/1/1882	*Bucephalus*	schooner	salted fish	Nantasket Beach
3/6/1883	*Alice G. Wonson*	schooner	fish	Harding's Ledge
2/17/1884	*Swordfish*	brig	lumber	Toddy Rocks
12/1/1885	*Anita Owen*	brig	coal	Nantasket Beach
1/9/1886	*Juliet*	schooner	granite	Deer Island
1/9/1886	*Millie Trim*	schooner	coal	Calf Island
7/20/1887	*Elmer E. Randall*	schooner	cod	Boston Lightship

Date	Name	Type	Cargo	Location
11/6/1888	*Goldsmith Maid*	schooner	fish	The Narrows
11/25/1888	*Cox & Green*	schooner	coal	Toddy Rocks
11/25/1888	*Gertrude Abbot*	schooner	coal	Toddy Rocks
11/25/1888	*Bertha F. Walker*	schooner	coal	Toddy Rocks
11/26/1888	*H. C. Higginson*	schooner	plaster	Nantasket Beach
11/26/1888	*Mattie E. Eaton*	schooner	ice/general	Nantasket Beach
11/26/1888	*Alice*	brig	sugar	Nantasket Beach
11/26/1888	*Avelon*	schooner	wood laths	Spectacle Island
1/21/1889	*H. F. Morse*	tug	–	Harding's Ledge
10/18/1890	*Louisa Smith*	schooner	cement	Broad Sound
11/5/1891	*Clara C. Cameron*	schooner	fish	Georges Island
8/26/1892	*Wm. S. Slater*	tug	–	Devil's Back Ledge
2/19/1893	*Enos B. Phillips*	schooner	coal	Harding's Ledge
2/22/1893	*Glenwood*	schooner	coal	Harding's Ledge
4/9/1894	*Mary A. Hood*	schooner	iron pipe	Nantasket Beach
2/2/1895	*Venetian*	steamer	cattle/sheep	Governor's Island
2/8/1895	*Mary Eliza*	schooner	baled hay	Deer Island
10/25/1895	*John F. Nickerson*	schooner	halibut	Castle Island
12/16/1896	*Ulrica*	schooner	plaster	Nantasket Beach
7/20/1897	*Elmer E. Randall*	schooner	cod	Boston Lightship
4/28/1898	*Cadet*	steamer	passengers	Deer Island
11/27/1898	*Abel E. Babcock*	schooner	coal	Stony Beach
11/27/1898	*Henry R. Tilton*	schooner	lumber	Toddy Rocks
11/27/1898	*Calvin F. Baker*	schooner	coal	Little Brewster Island
11/27/1898	*Virginia*	schooner	wax	Thompson's Island
1/3/1900	*Resolute*	tug	–	Governor's Island
2/25/1900	*Keystone*	schooner	coal	Shag Rocks
9/16/1900	*John Endicott*	steamer	–	Harding's Ledge
10/7/1901	*Columbia*	schooner	cod/haddock	Lighthouse Channel
10/21/1903	*J. B. King Co. #17*	schooner	cement	Harding's Ledge
12/29/1903	*Kiowa*	steamer	cotton/oranges	Outer Harbor
1/3/1904	*Belle J. Neal*	schooner	salt fish	Point Allerton
3/13/1904	*City of Boston*	steamer	(ferryboat)	East Boston
7/3/1905	*Chromo*	schooner	in ballast	Outer Harbor
3/20/1906	*C. H. Lane*	schooner	clay	Little Brewster Island
4/4/1906	*Wyalusing*	tug	–	Harding's Ledge
11/15/1906	*Mary Lee Newton*	schooner	coal	False Spit Bar
1/24/1907	*A. H. Heaton*	schooner	lime	Outer Harbor
11/4/1907	*City of Birmingham*	steamer	general	Castle Island
1/24/1908	*Fortuna*	schooner	in ballast	Lovell's Island

Date	Name	Type	Cargo	Location
11/21/1908	*Hugh G.*	schooner	plaster	Outer Harbor
12/26/1909	*Davis Palmer*	schooner	coal	Broad Sound
10/1/1911	*M. H. Read*	schooner	lumber	Lovell's Island
7/14/1913	*Alberta*	sloop	passengers	Outer Harbor
1/1/1914	*John J. Fallon*	schooner	halibut/flounder	False Spit Bar
9/9/1914	*R. L. Tay*	schooner	lumber	Long Island
10/20/1914	*Anne Perry*	schooner	flounder/cod	Outer Harbor
9/9/1916	*Marguerite*	schooner	moulding sand	South Boston
8/11/1917	*Mayflower*	steamer	passengers	Spectacle Island
9/24/1924	*Edward Peirce*	steamer	coal	South Boston
9/26/1924	*Actor*	schooner	fish	Broad Sound
2/20/1927	*Nancy*	schooner	in ballast	Nantasket Beach
2/13/1928	*Mohave*	tug	–	Harding's Ledge
9/9/1936	*Romance*	steamer	passengers	Outer Harbor
4/22/1938	*City of Salisbury*	steamer	zoo animals/rubber	Outer Harbor
1/21/1941	*Mary E. O'Hara*	schooner	fish	Outer Harbor
11/29/1951	*Lynn*	trawler	fish	Outer Harbor
6/22/1955	*Pilgrim Belle*	steamer	passengers	Spectacle Island

NOTE: Locations are approximate. Hundreds of incidents have occurred in Boston Harbor. These listings are for wrecks reported under headings in this book only and are intended to generally indicate a statistical sampling.

Major Wrecks by Location

Boston Lightship	2	Lovell's Island	4
Broad Sound	3	Lower Middle Shoal	1
Calf Island	1	Middle Brewster Island	1
Castle Island	2	Nantasket Beach	17
Charlestown	2	Neponset River	1
Chelsea	1	Outer Brewster Island	2
Deer Island	11	Outer Harbor	10
Devil's Back Ledge	2	Peddock's Island	1
East Boston	1	Point Allerton	10
False Spit Bar	2	Rainsford Island	1
Gallop's Island	1	Shag Rocks	7
Georges Island	2	South Boston	1
Governor's Island	3	Spectacle Island	3
Harding's Ledge	12	Stony Beach	3
Hull Gut	1	The Narrows	1
Lighthouse Channel	1	Thompson's Island	1
Little Brewster Island	4	Toddy Rocks	5
Long Island	1		

Alfred Hale & Co.

MANUFACTURERS OF AND DEALERS IN

Rubber Goods

—AND—

SUBMARINE

Diving Apparatus

26 SCHOOL ST.

BOSTON, MASS.

DAVID HALE.

ANDREW J. MORSE & SON,

Fire Department Supplies

SUB-MARINE ARMOR.

— THE BEST —

DIVING APPARATUS

IN USE.

Adopted by the U. S. Government and the leading Wrecking Co's and divers.

COMPLETE OUTFITS

Always on Hand.

— MANUFACTURERS OF —

HOSE COUPLINGS, HOSE PIPES, HYDRANT GATES, SIAMESE CONNECTIONS, Etc.

SEND FOR PRICE LIST.

140 Congress Street, Boston.

GEO. W. TOWNSEND,

DIVER, ENGINEER & CONTRACTOR

FOR DREDGING.

202 Atlantic Av., foot of State St., Boston

Recovery of any sunken property; construction, inspection, and repair of dams, piers, abutments and submerged foundations, sea walls, coffer dams; blasting and removal of sunken rocks, wrecks, and obstructions; laying of submerged pipes; examination of docks, vessels' bottoms; clearing fouled propellers; marine railways; steam pumps, wrecking tugs, lighters and wrecking appliances in readiness. As many drowning accidents occur in every locality, I desire to call your attention to the invaluable utility of the Submarine Diving Armor for the sure and prompt recovery of drowned persons. I have a staff of experienced, reliable Divers, fully equipped, and ready to proceed at once to the scene of disaster. Do not permit the inhuman and brutal practice of using barbed hooks and pointed grapplings which lacerate the flesh and mutilate the remains. Telegraph without delay as soon as the accident occurs.

Diving Advertisement, Boston Directory of late 1800s

Major Wrecks by Month

January	16
February	18
March	11
April	7
May	3
June	2
July	5
August	4
September	8
October	8
November	22
December	15
Unknown	2

SEIZINGS, HITCHES, BENDS, SPLICES, Etc.

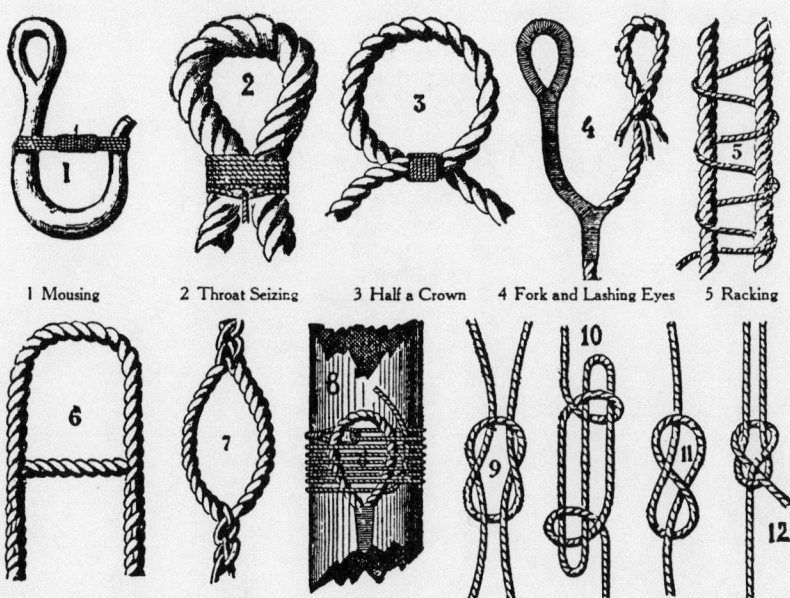

1 Mousing   2 Throat Seizing   3 Half a Crown   4 Fork and Lashing Eyes   5 Racking

6 Horse Shoe Splice 7 Cut Splice 8 Rose Lashing 9 Reef Knot 10 Sheep Shank 11 Figure of Eight Knot 12 Single Bend

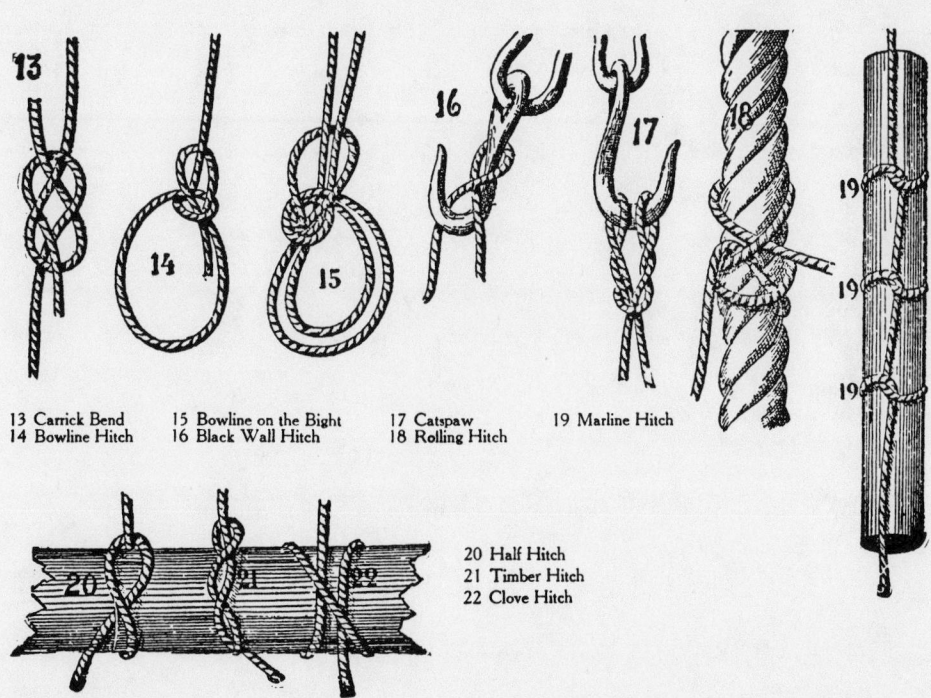

13 Carrick Bend   15 Bowline on the Bight   17 Catspaw   19 Marline Hitch
14 Bowline Hitch   16 Black Wall Hitch   18 Rolling Hitch

20 Half Hitch
21 Timber Hitch
22 Clove Hitch

Major Wrecks
by Type of Cargo

animals	2	hemp	1
baled hay	1	ice	1
beer	1	in ballast	4
brandy	1	iron	2
cannon	1	leather	1
cement	2	lumber products	8
cigars	2	miscellaneous	19*
clay	1	molasses	2
coal	16	oranges	1
coffee	3	passengers	10
cotton	2	plaster	4
eggs	1	rum	1
fish	17	silks	1
flour	2	sugar	3
general	7	wax	1
gin	1	wool	1
granite	1		

* Miscellaneous includes combination cargos, 4 man-o'-war, 1 pilot boat, and 6 tugs.

Major Wrecks by Type of Vessel

—⚓—

Bark	3
Brig	22
Ferryboat	1
Man-o'-war	4
Pilot boat	1
Schooner	60
Ship (full-rigged)	8
Sloop	2
Steamer	11
Trawler	1
Tug	6
Unknown	2

Government List of Wrecks
Prior to World War II

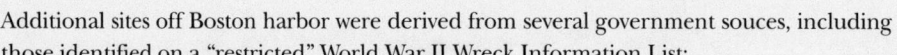

Additional sites off Boston harbor were derived from several government souces, including those identified on a "restricted" World War II Wreck Information List:

Name	Type	Date	Location
Herbert	steam lighter	8/7/1924	LAT. 42° 25' 05"N LONG. 70° 51' 25"W
McGowan	lighter	8/8/1930	LAT. 42° 21' 10"N LONG. 70° 43' 00"W
Ethel N.	schooner	12/31/1930	LAT. 42° 22' 45"N LONG. 70° 39' 30"W
Massasoit	steamer	1/22/1931	LAT. 42° 24' 26"N LONG. 70° 39' 00"W
Eagle Boat #42	patrol	6/15/1931	LAT. 42° 22' 26"N LONG. 70° 43' 23"W
C. H. Sprague	tug	10/5/1931	LAT. 42° 20' 24"N LONG. 70° 40' 47"W
Blue Jay	tug	10/10/1931	LAT. 42° 20' 56"N LONG. 70° 41' 05"W
Dredge #6	–	10/10/1931	LAT. 42° 20' 56"N LONG. 70° 41' 05"W
Dredge #9	–	10/20/1931	LAT. 42° 21' 45"N LONG. 70° 41' 20"W
Coyote	steamer	1/11/1932	LAT. 42° 22' 06"N LONG. 70° 43' 06"W
Unidentifed	lighter	5/26/1932	LAT. 42° 22' 06" LONG. 70° 43' 06"W
Cornelia	tug	7/8/1933	LAT. 42° 23' 05"N LONG. 70° 45' 05"W

Name	Type	Date	Location
Reliance	lighter	8/3/1933	LAT. 42° 21' 25"N LONG. 70° 42' 00"W
King Philip	steam packet	4/7/1935	LAT. 42° 22' 03"N LONG. 70° 37' 11"W
Beatrice	tug	4/27/1935	LAT. 42° 21' 25"N LONG. 70° 42' 15"W
Evans	lighter	6/28/1935	LAT. 42° 21' 00"N LONG. 70° 42' 50"W
Roxanna	steam yacht	9/10/1935	LAT. 42° 20' 39"N LONG. 70° 40' 43"W
Annie Conant	lighter	4/1/1936	LAT. 42° 21' 45"N LONG. 70° 39' 05"W
Mist	trawler	4/8/1936	LAT. 42° 23' 36"N LONG. 70° 39' 18"W
Romance	steamer	9/9/1936	LAT. 42° 23' 43"N LONG. 70° 51' 46"W
Wave	trawler	9/21/1936	LAT. 42° 22' 45"N LONG. 70° 39' 25"W
Gale	trawler	4/27/1937	LAT. 42° 26' 04"N LONG. 70° 37' 33"W
Ocean	trawler	4/26/1938	LAT. 42° 23' 19"N LONG. 70° 35' 33"W
Vesta	tug	4/26/1938	LAT. 42° 21' 50"N LONG. 70° 39' 48"W
Wm. H. Yerkes, Jr.	tug	4/26/1938	LAT. 42° 21' 50"N LONG. 70° 39' 48"W
City of Salisbury	freighter	5/22/1938	LAT. 42° 22' 26"N LONG. 70° 51' 35"W
Joel Cook	lighter	8/18/1938	LAT. 42° 21' 45"N LONG. 70° 40' 25"W
Mary A. White	sloop	7/1/1940	LAT. 42° 23' 30"N LONG. 70° 40' 25"W
Confidence	tug	11/5/1940	LAT. 42° 24' 30"N LONG. 70° 39' 05"W

Plotting of these wrecks during World War II was important to the U.S. Navy in conducting antisubmarine operations. Most of these vessels were disposed of in the so-called dumping ground. Furthermore, specific areas were designated for discarding explosives and ordnance.

SOURCES

For those readers interested in further research, as well as for those fascinated by reading original accounts of shipwrecks, the following is a partial list of primary sources used to gather the information contained in this book.

Prologue

Anne Kinnear, chariman, Hull Historical Commission

Boston Post

Glouster Daily Times

Sidney Perley. *Historic Storms of New England,* 1891.

Massachusetts Humane Society Records

Port of Boston Marine Journal

General Descrition of Harbor

Bird's Eye View of Boston Harbor, Walker Lithograph Co., Boston.

Bird's Eye View of Boston Harbor and South Shore to Provincetown Showing Steamboat Routes, Union News Co., Boston.

Boston Illustrated, James R. Osgood & Co., 1872.

Descriptive and Historical Sketch of Boston Harbor and Surroundings, 1855.

Samuel G. Drake. *History and Antiquities of Boston,* 1857.

James H. Stark. *Illustrated History of Boston Harbor,* 1879.

M.F. Sweetser. *King's Handbook of Boston Harbor,* 1889.

Memorial History of Boston Harbor, James R. Osgood & Co., 1880.

Nathaniel B. Shurtleff. *Topographical and Historical Description of Boston,* 1890.

U.S. Coast and Geodetic Survey charts and records

A Witch's Brew of Hazards

Boston Advertiser

Boston Transcript

Nathaniel B. Shurtleff. *Topographical and Historical Description of Boston,* 1891.

U.S. Coast and Geodetic Survey charts and records

Pirates and Treasure

Archivo Historico - Madrid Nacional

Boston Newsletter

National Archives - General Services Administration

U.S. Department of the Treasury

Harbor Phenomena

The Boston Globe

Boston Post

Boston Transcript

Boston Traveler

Historical Flotsam and Jetsam

Boston Journal

The Boston Globe

Bostonian Society Publications, Old State House, Boston

M.F. Sweetser. *King's Handbook of Boston Harbor,* 1889.

A Tongue-in-Cheek Meeting on Wrecks

James Lloyd Homer. *Notes on the Sea Shore,* 1848.

Samaritans of the Coast

Samuel G. Drake. *History and Antiquities of Boston,* 1857.

Massachusetts Humane Society Records

Fitz-Henry Smith, Jr. *Storms and Shipwrecks in Boston Bay and the Record of the Life Savers of Hull,* 1918.

U.S. Life Saving Service Records

U.S. Coast Guard Records

Catastrophic Nineteenth-century Storms

The Boston Globe

Gloucester Telegram

Gloucester Times

Harper's Monthly

Judeth Van Hamm, director, Hull Lifesaving Museum

Quincy Daily Ledger

Fitz-Henry Smith, Jr. *Storms and Shipwrecks in Boston Bay and the Record of the Life Savers of Hull,* 1918.

The Outer Harbor

E. and G. W. Blunt. *American Coast Pilot*

The Boston Daily Globe

Boston Evening Transcript

The Boston Globe

Boston Herald

Boston Morning Post

Boston Post

Dennis Means, curator, The Means Library, Hull

Higham Journal

Higham Journal and Advertiser

James H. Stark. *Illustrated History of Boston Harbor,* 1879.

M. F. Sweetser. *King's Handbook of Boston Harbor,* 1889.

Marine Journal

Massachusetts Humane Society Records

Merchants Exchange Book

James Lloyd Homer. *Note on the Sea Shores,* 1848.

Palmer's News Room Book
Richard M. Boonisar, authority on Lifesaving
Richard Francis Cleverly, president, Hull Historical Society
U.S. Coast and Geodetic Survey Charts and Records
U. S. Life Saving Records

Middle-Islands Shipwrecks

John H. Fenton. *Battle of Boston Harbor,* 1946.
Boston Daily Advertiser
Boston Daily Advertiser Marine Journal
The Boston Globe
Boston Post
Boston Post Marine Journal
A. Bowen. *Bowen's Picture of Boston,* 1829.
M. F. Sweetser. *King's Handbook of Boston Harbor,* 1889.
Massachusetts Humane Society Records
Salem Gazette
U.S. Coast and Geodetic Survey Charts and Records
U.S. Life Saving Service Records
U.S. Navy Department Records

Boston and Inner-Islands Shipwrecks

Boston Advertiser
The Boston Globe
Boston Journal
Boston Post
Boston Transcript
Patrick J. Connelly. *Islands of Boston Harbor,* 1936.
Massachusetts Humane Society Records
Proceedings of the Bostonian Society Old State House, Boston
U.S. Coast and Geodetic Survey Charts and Records
U.S. Life Saving Service Records